Best Practices for Therapy
Empirically Based Treatment Protocols

Dear Mental Health Professional:

This protocol is part of the *Best Practices for Therapy* Series that is designed to provide mental health practitioners empirically based treatment programs. We have edited this series to be clear and user-friendly, yet comprehensive and step-by-step.

The series offers high quality, consistently formatted protocols that include everything you need to initiate and complete treatment. Each session is outlined in detail with its own agenda, client education materials, and skill-building interventions. Each session also provides sample instructions and therapist-client dialogues.

The therapist protocol you are using corresponds with an available client manual that is designed to be used concurrently. Your protocol has all the worksheets, homework assignments, in-session treatment exercises, and didactic material that is in the client manual. Also included are pre- and post-assessments, and an overall program evaluation. An appendix contains a treatment plan summary (now required by many managed care companies).

Ten *Best Practices for Therapy* protocols are currently available or in development. They include protocols for PTSD, GAD, OCD, agoraphobia/panic disorder, specific phobia, social phobia, depression, anger management, BPD, and eating disorders.

We wish you every success in using this program with your clients.

Sincerely,

Matthew McKay, Ph.D.
John Preston, Psy.D.
Carole Honeychurch, M.A.

OVERCOMING POST-TRAUMATIC STRESS DISORDER

■

A Cognitive-Behavioral
Exposure-Based Protocol
for the Treatment of PTSD
and the Other Anxiety Disorders

Larry Smyth, Ph.D.

Best Practices for Therapy
Empirically Based Treatment Protocols

Publisher's Note

This publication is designed to provide accurate and authoritative information in regard to the subject matter covered. It is sold with the understanding that the publisher is not engaged in rendering psychological, financial, legal, or other professional services. If expert assistance or counseling is needed, the services of a competent professional should be sought.

Distributed in Canada by Raincoast Books

Copyright © 1999 by Larry Smyth, Ph.D.
           New Harbinger Publications, Inc.
           5674 Shattuck Avenue
           Oakland, CA 94609

Cover design by Poulson\Gluck Design.
Edited by Donna Latte.
Text design by Michele Waters.

Library of Congress Catalog Card Number: 98-67411

ISBN-10 1-57224-162-4
ISBN-13 978-1-57224-162-6

All Rights Reserved

Printed in the United States of America

New Harbinger Publications' website address: www.newharbinger.com

09   08   07

10   9   8   7   6   5   4   3

Contents

Introduction   1

Phase I   **Assessment and Goal Setting**   21
Sessions 1 and 2

Phase II   **Emotion-Focused Coping-Skills Training**   33
Sessions 3 and 4

Phase III   **Assimilation Work**   47
Session 5

Phase IV   **Brief Exposure and Assimilation Work**   63
Sessions 6 to 11

Phase V   **Prolonged Exposure and Assimilation Work**   75
Sessions 12 and 13

Phase VI   **Relapse Prevention Work**   87
Sessions 14 and 15

Appendix A   **Theory**   91

Appendix B   **Modified PTSD Symptom Scale**   97

Appendix C   **Smyth's *Complete Home-Study Course***   101

Appendix D   **Resources**   103

Appendix E   **Treatment Plan**   105

Works Cited   107

Introduction

This manual is intended for all mental-health professionals who are in a position to treat posttraumatic stress disorder (PTSD). This is likely to include psychologists, psychiatrists, social workers, counselors, clergy, and psychiatric nurses. The cognitive-behavioral exposure-based approach presented in this manual normally requires a commitment of between ten and fifteen weekly sessions in the case of simple PTSD. Complex PTSD usually requires a somewhat greater commitment.

The approach, labeled the TAB-P treatment protocol, emphasizes the importance of establishing a therapeutic relationship (T) and applying assimilation (A) or cognitive reframing strategies to reduce the dissonance created by information contained in a PTSD client's traumatic memories that contradicts the client's overarching beliefs about the world and themselves—for example, a child's death that cannot be reconciled with a PTSD client's belief in a just and predictable world. Finally, the approach emphasizes the importance of integrating and applying two forms of exposure: brief exposure (B) and prolonged exposure (P). (I will provide a more detailed discussion of brief exposure and prolonged exposure later in this manual.)

This approach presumes that the mental-health professional is at least somewhat familiar with cognitive-behavioral exposure techniques and cognitive-behavioral reframing strategies. Those unfamiliar with these techniques probably will require some additional training before they will be able to successfully apply them. Such training is available in a home-study course (see appendix C for details).

Overview of the Disorder

Major Clinical Features

The fourth edition of the *Diagnostic and Statistical Manual of Mental Disorders* (1994), or *DSM-IV*, organizes the diagnostic features of PTSD in terms of the following six criteria (the major clinical features are italicized):

1. the individual must have been *exposed to a traumatic event* that involved actual or threatened death or serious injury of self or others, to which they responded with intense fear, helplessness, or horror;

2. they must *persistently reexperience the traumatic event* in the form of intrusive thoughts, nightmares, flashbacks, intense psychological and/or physiological distress upon exposure to internal or external cues that symbolize or resemble an aspect of the traumatic event;

3. they must *persistently avoid stimuli* associated with the trauma, and/or they must experience a numbing of general emotional responsiveness;

4. they must experience *persistent symptoms of hyperarousal* such as an exaggerated startle reflex;

5. the duration of the reexperiencing, avoidance/numbing, and hyperarousal symptoms must be at least one month; and

6. the symptoms must cause the individual clinically significant distress or impairment in psychosocial functioning.

Subtypes

The *DSM-IV* goes on to differentiate between acute PTSD, wherein the duration of the symptoms is more than one month but less than three months, and chronic PTSD, wherein the duration is greater than three months. If the onset of symptoms is at least six months after the traumatic event, then the PTSD is additionally designated as having delayed onset. There is growing recognition among mental health professionals that PTSD should have two additional subtypes—simple PTSD and complex PTSD—although these are not recognized as distinct subtypes in the *DSM-IV*. Complex PTSD is also sometimes referred to as "disorders of extreme stress not otherwise specified." These two subtypes are thought to differ in terms of their symptom constellation, with simple PTSD fitting the *DSM-IV* criteria for PTSD described above, and complex PTSD presenting several additional symptom clusters. These clusters include somatic symptoms, dissociation, severe affect regulation dysfunction approaching that seen in bipolar and borderline personality disorders, and pervasive interpersonal relationship difficulties (Herman 1992, 1993; Newman, Riggs, and Roth 1997). These two subtypes are also thought to differ in terms of their etiology. Simple PTSD is thought to arise from acute time-limited traumas (disaster, rape, auto accident), whereas complex PTSD is thought to arise out of prolonged severe trauma that is purposely perpetrated by mankind (prisoner of war experiences, prolonged torture conditions, sustained childhood sexual abuse, severe and prolonged combat). The prognosis for complex PTSD is thought to be substantially worse than that for simple PTSD. Rather than two dichotomous subtypes, there may well be a continuum from simple PTSD to complex PTSD. More and more of the complex PTSD symptom clusters probably become manifest as the degree and duration of the life-threat increase, as the malevolence of the human perpetrator increases, and as the age at which the victimization occurs decreases.

Prevalence

Community-based studies suggest that approximately three-quarters of the general population in the United States have been exposed to one or more life-threatening traumatic event(s) in their lifetime (Kilpatrick and Resnick 1993). Of those so exposed, about a quarter of the individuals go on to develop full-blown PTSD, with the rates varying considerably depending on the nature and duration of the exposure (Green 1994). For example, rape victims were found to develop PTSD 80 percent of the time in one study (Breslau et al. 1991) and 35 percent of the time in another study (Kilpatrick and Resnick 1993). Vietnam veterans were found to have lifetime PTSD prevalence rates of 31 percent (Kulka et al. 1990). Prisoners of war held by the Japanese in World War II were found to have lifetime prevalence rates of 50 percent (Speed et al. 1991). Accident victims were found to have lifetime prevalence rates of 12 percent (Breslau et al. 1991; Norris 1992). Current PTSD community prevalence rates for full PTSD and partial PTSD generally are thought to range from between 6 percent and 9 percent (for a more thorough review, see Green 1994).

Etiology

By definition, experiences that have a significant threat of serious bodily harm or death to oneself or others are the primary etiological agent in PTSD. The more severe, prolonged, and unexpected the life threat, the more the life threat arises from human rather than natural causes, and the greater the malevolence of the human perpetrator, the greater the likelihood that the traumatic events will produce PTSD. Also, the more the life-threatening experiences contradict the exposed individuals' most valued assumptions about the world (such as beliefs in a just and loving God or beliefs in a just and orderly world), the greater the likelihood that the experiences will produce PTSD. Similarly, the more that life-threatening experiences induce individuals to think, feel, or behave in ways that contradict their most valued assumptions about themselves (such as experiencing intense homicidal rage or engaging in self-defensive behavior that is morally unacceptable), the greater the likelihood that the experiences will produce PTSD (Smyth 1994a; Horowitz 1986; Foa and Riggs 1993).

Several predisposing psychological variables appear to play significant causal roles in the etiology of PTSD as well, including low intellectual ability (McNally and Shin 1995; Kulka et al. 1990) and genetic factors (True et al. 1993; McFarlane 1989). Conversely, high levels of social support after traumatic events appear to buffer the effects of trauma and reduce the probability that PTSD will develop (Soloman and Smith 1994). Although these nontrauma-related variables are not as critical to the development of PTSD as is the trauma itself, these variables do account for substantial variance in the etiology of PTSD when they are taken as a whole (Yehuda and McFarlane 1994). These nontrauma-related variables also probably influence whether simple PTSD or complex PTSD will develop from a given traumatic experience, and they also probably influence the spontaneous remission rates of the PTSD that can develop. Overall, approximately 50 percent of all PTSD appears to spontaneously remit over the course of time with the majority of this remission taking place within the first two years posttrauma (Kulka et al. 1990; Green 1994; Breslau et al. 1998.). That is, the PTSD symptoms resolve to the point that the *DSM* criteria are no longer met, and this occurs without the intervention of a mental health professional. See Meichenbaum (1994) for a more thorough discussion of the etiology of PTSD.

Essential Elements of the TAB-P Protocol

Theory

The TAB-P treatment is a cognitive-behavioral exposure-based approach to treating PTSD and other anxiety disorders. The TAB-P protocol proposes that five variables account for the vast majority of the variance in treatment outcomes with these disorders. More specifically, the quality and type of the therapeutic relationship (T), the application of assimilation (A) or cognitive reframing strategies, the application of brief-exposure strategies (B), and the application of prolonged-exposure strategies (P) are four variables thought to strongly influence treatment outcomes. A fifth variable, the complexity of the clinical picture (C), is also recognized as an important variable that moderates the effects of the other variables. The theory as a whole can be succinctly expressed by way of the following analysis of variance metaphor:

treatment outcome is a function of = C(.2T + .2TA + .4TB + .2TP).

There are several important implications to this theory. First, a collaborative therapeutic relationship coupled with the client perceiving the therapist as a trustworthy, understanding, competent, and caring individual are considered necessary but not sufficient conditions for good treatment outcomes. However, the so-called nonspecific effects of establishing a collaborative and supportive therapeutic relationship with clients and providing them with a credible treatment rationale are thought to be sufficient to produce fair treatment outcomes with simple PTSD and other uncomplicated anxiety disorders. Second, the application of assimilation strategies, the application of brief-exposure strategies, and the application of prolonged-exposure strategies all interact with the quality of the therapeutic relationship in determining outcomes in the treatment of PTSD and other anxiety disorders. Third, assimilation strategies, brief-exposure strategies, and prolonged-exposure strategies each contribute something to treatment outcomes in their own right and do so independently of one another. Fourth, the application of brief exposure-strategies accounts for more variance in treatment outcomes than do assimilation strategies or prolonged-exposure strategies, which are equivalent in influencing treatment outcomes. Fifth, the complexity of the clinical picture moderates the influence of these other four variables. That is, outcomes will be better in the TAB-P treatment of uncomplicated simple PTSD than they will be in the TAB-P treatment of either complex PTSD or in the TAB-P treatment of simple PTSD that is compounded by severe comorbidity. This also holds true in the TAB-P treatment of other anxiety disorders that are compounded by severe comorbidity (for a more detailed discussion of this theory, see appendix A).

The Therapeutic Relationship

The therapeutic relationship can be construed as a continuum with one end anchored by a collaborative relationship between client and therapist, with the client perceiving the therapist as a caring, trustworthy expert capable of assisting him or her in reaching mutually agreed-upon treatment goals. At the other end of the continuum is a relationship characterized by the therapist being perceived as an omnipotent being who prescribes treatments to a submissive, passive, subordinate client. PTSD treatment outcomes are maximized when the established therapeutic relationship is toward the collaborative and supportive end of the continuum, and the therapist can empathetically listen to a client recount their tragedy and can do so in a supportive manner without becoming unduly distressed by the horror of the client's story. The obverse of this skill is for the therapist to listen to a client's tragedy in an aloof, unconcerned, unsympathetic, or critical fashion. This proposition parallels many of those made by Carl Rogers (1957) some time ago. The witnessing of the client's trauma in a safe, supportive relationship can also be found in the writings of existential therapists such as Frankl (1959), and more recently in the writings of a host of contemporary theorists operating from a variety of theoretical perspectives. Despite the confluence of thought on this matter from many diverse sources, there is virtually no empirical data substantiating any of it with respect to PTSD. There is, however, a great deal of empirical evidence supporting the notion of the importance of the therapeutic relationship in psychotherapy outcomes in general (Whiston and Sexton 1993; Beutler et al. 1994; Weinberger 1995). Besides, there simply is no credible reason to believe that the quality of the therapeutic relationship doesn't have as substantial an effect on psychotherapy outcomes in the treatment of PTSD as it does in the treatment of other disorders.

The Assessment Process

The foundation for a collaborative and supportive therapeutic relationship is generally laid in the assessment process. Thus, the instruments used in this process should appear credible to the client and should be administered in a flexible, client-friendly manner. Interviews conducted by the treating clinician are preferred over other assessment instruments since the interview process more readily lends itself to establishing a supportive and collaborative therapeutic relationship than do other assessment devices. Brief paper-and-pencil instruments that have good face validity can also be used, provided the client is given a credible rationale for taking them. Scheduling the client to take a time-consuming battery of tests with little or no rationale being provided for them, and then having the tests administered by an indifferent technician who will not be treating the client, are all-too-common assessment practices that should be avoided.

Treatment Goals

The setting of treatment goals usually follows on the heels of the assessment process. If done properly, the setting of treatment goals should reinforce and strengthen the establishment of a supportive and collaborative therapeutic relationship. The treatment goals that are set must not only take into account the client's presenting complaints, they must also take into account the severity and type of any comorbidity that may exist, the severity of any contemporary psychosocial stressors that are impinging on the client, and the client's expectations. Probably the best way to accomplish this is to briefly summarize what is found in the assessment phase and then propose a tentative treatment plan that is refined and finalized in collaboration with the client.

Treatment Rationale

Presenting the client with a credible treatment rationale usually occurs once the treatment goals have been agreed upon. If done properly, this should reinforce the supportive and collaborative nature of the therapeutic relationship. It should also help create favorable and realistic expectations in the client, which has been shown in a number of studies to significantly increase the chances of positive psychotherapy outcomes with a variety of mental health disorders (Garfield 1994). Probably the best way to accomplish this is to educate the client in a straightforward manner as to the principles of treating PTSD by way of exposure strategies and assimilation strategies. Paraphrasing the educational material pertaining to these concepts found in the accompanying client manual is a good way of accomplishing this. The client should also be given a homework assignment to read about these concepts in the client manual between sessions. This not only reinforces the educational endeavors of the therapist but also lays the groundwork for future homework assignments.

Exposure Strategies

The TAB-P protocol emphasizes the importance of integrating and applying two forms of exposure: brief exposure and prolonged exposure. The prolonged-exposure strategy presented here is derived from contemporary approaches (such as Foa et al. 1993) as well as from the older approaches of implosion (Stampf and Levis 1967) and flooding (Keane et al. 1985). The brief-exposure strategy presented here is derived from several graduated exposure approaches, including Wolpe's (1958) systematic desensitization and William's (1990) guided mastery, as well as Meichenbaum's (1985) stress inoculation training. The brief-exposure strategy in this manual incorporates three client-directed emotion-focused coping skills: the eye-movement technique, the relaxation response, and rational thinking. Clients are taught to combine these three coping skills to reduce moderate levels of distress produced by gradual exposure to their feared stimulus complexes. Clients progressively move from imaginal exposure to in vivo exposure as they simultaneously progress from brief exposure to prolonged exposure. Prolonged exposure is introduced only after strong coping effects and a sense of mastery have both accrued by way of the brief-exposure strategy. In this way, the superior desensitization properties and relatively low relapse rates of prolonged exposure can be retained without incurring the adverse treatment outcomes that sometimes accompany the use of prolonged exposure.

Assimilation and Other Cognitive-Reframing Strategies

Assimilation and other cognitive-reframing strategies are employed to reduce the dissonance created by information contained in a PTSD client's traumatic memories that contradicts the client's overarching beliefs about the world and themselves. Assimilation strategies have much in common with rational-thinking strategies popularized by Ellis (1975) and Beck (1976). Both types of cognitive-reframing strategies utilize metaphors, Socratic questioning, and straightforward didactic maneuvers to help clients correct their pathogenic appraisals and underlying beliefs regarding themselves and their world. Assimilation strategies tend to have a more philosophical appearance and more often target clients' overarching beliefs than do rational thinking strategies, which tend to more often target clients' specific appraisals.

Treating Other Anxiety Disorders

The TAB-P protocol is a very cost-effective form of psychotherapy since it readily lends itself to the treatment of all the anxiety disorders, not just PTSD (Smyth 1994a). All that is required is to focus the application of the integrated exposure strategies of the TAB-P protocol on different aspects of the feared stimulus complex, depending on which of the anxiety disorders is being treated. In the case of a simple phobia, external visual stimuli coupled with catastrophic appraisals of grave physical harm are the aspects of the client's feared stimulus complex most often responsible for provoking his or her excessive anxiety. In the case of a social phobia, external visual stimuli coupled with catastrophic appraisals of humiliation and grave social harm are the aspects of the client's feared stimulus complex most often responsible for provoking his or her excessive anxiety. In the case of panic disorder, unusual somatic sensations coupled with catastrophic appraisals of grave physical and grave social harm are the aspects of the client's feared stimulus complex most often responsible for provoking his or her excessive anxiety. In the case of a generalized anxiety disorder, worry and automatic thoughts predicting catastrophic physical harm to oneself and others are the aspects of the client's feared stimulus complex most often responsible for provoking his or her excessive anxiety.

Compartmentalization-of-worry strategies (Smyth 1994a) often need to be added to the integrated exposure strategies of the TAB-P protocol when treating generalized anxiety disorders in order to maximize the chances of good treatment outcomes with this disorder. In the case of obsessive-compulsive disorder, external visual stimuli coupled with catastrophic appraisals of physical harm to oneself or others are the aspects of the client's feared stimulus complex most often responsible for provoking his or her excessive anxiety. This, in turn, drives the obsessive-compulsive disordered client's repetitive thoughts and behaviors, which are temporarily reassuring. Response-prevention strategies that obstruct the client's compulsive behavior often need to be added to the integrated exposure strategies of the TAB-P protocol when treating obsessive-compulsive disorder in order to maximize the chances of good treatment outcomes with this disorder. In the case of PTSD, internal visual images related to their traumatic memories coupled with catastrophic appraisals of physical harm to oneself or others are the aspects of the client's feared stimulus complex most often responsible for provoking his or her excessive anxiety.

Group Therapy

The TAB-P protocol can be delivered in group therapy settings to a wide variety of mental health problems to include all of the anxiety disorders, the mood disorders, and substance abuse disorders that are in remission but at risk for relapse due to poor affect management. Even the anxiety-based symptoms in psychotic disorders (panic attacks triggered by unusual somatic sensations as well as phobias and generalized anxiety related to worry about thought-disorder symptoms) can be treated by way of the TAB-P protocol in group settings, provided the clients have been stabilized on the appropriate medications. The thought-disorder symptoms of such clients must not be so severe as to disrupt the group and/or preclude learning, however. When delivered in group settings, the fifteen-session TAB-P format should be broken down into three phases—a five-session basic training phase, a five-session advanced training phase, and a five-session graduate training phase. In the basic training phase, participants should be trained to use the eye-movement technique, the relaxation response, and rational thinking as emotion-focused coping skills. They should also be introduced to three critical concepts—the Serenity Prayer, the CAP principle, and the SUD scale. The Serenity Prayer encourages participants to adopt a philosophy of "change those things you can change, accept those things you cannot change, and be very good at figuring out which is which." The CAP principle provides participants with a strategy for applying the emotion-focused coping skills they have been taught (see the chapter entitled Phase IV for a more detailed explanation of this acronym). The SUD scale is simply a scale that participants use to rate their subjective units of emotional distress when applying the CAP principle in their exposure work (the SUD scale is presented in this introduction under the section entitled "Self-Rating Scales.") Once the clients have been trained in the three emotion-focused coping skills and introduced to the three critical concepts, they should be introduced to imaginal brief-exposure work in the group setting wherein they practice applying these coping skills. Throughout the basic training phase, participants should be encouraged to experiment with the application of the three emotion-focused coping skills on their own, outside the group sessions. Upon satisfactory completion of the basic training phase, clients can elect to move into the advanced training phase, where more imaginal brief-exposure work is conducted and assigned as homework, and in vivo brief-exposure work is begun. Upon satisfactory completion of the advanced training phase, clients can elect to move on to the graduate training phase. In this phase, the clients continue with their imaginal brief-exposure work and with their in vivo brief-exposure work. In addition, they move on to conducting imaginal prolonged-exposure work and in vivo prolonged-exposure work. The basic training phase can be conducted with large heterogeneous groups of clients, but the advanced and graduate phases should be conducted with smaller, more homogeneous groups of clients to better monitor the clients' exposure work as well as facilitate group cohesiveness.

Research

Considerable empirical evidence has accrued substantiating the efficacy of exposure strategies in the treatment of all the anxiety disorders, including phobias (Heimberg 1993), panic disorder (Acierno et al. 1993; Clum et al. 1993), obsessive-compulsive disorder (Foa 1996), generalized anxiety disorder (Chambless and Gillis 1993), and PTSD (Foa and Rothbaum 1989; Soloman et al. 1992; Van Etten and Taylor 1998). There is even a small but growing body of empirical evidence supporting the efficacy of integrating brief-exposure and prolonged-exposure strategies when treating PTSD (Cohen and Mannarino 1996; Deblinger et al. 1990; Stauffer and Deblinger 1996). Deblinger and Heflin's book (1996) details the treatment of PTSD in children using such an approach. Sufficient empirical evidence has now accrued that brief-exposure strategies and prolonged-exposure strategies have both been deemed "probably efficacious treatment" for PTSD by the Task Force for the Promotion and Dissemination of Empirically Validated Psychotherapies (Chambless et al. 1998). This taskforce found no other psychotherapies more efficacious than exposure strategies in the treatment of PTSD. It also deemed exposure strategies "efficacious" in the treatment of phobias, panic disorder, obsessive-compulsive disorder, and generalized anxiety disorder. This ongoing taskforce was founded in the early 1990s by the Clinical Psychology Division of the American Psychological Association.

The empirical evidence that has accumulated supporting the efficacy of eye-movement desensitization and reprocessing, or EMDR (Shapiro 1989, 1995), in the treatment of simple PTSD probably deserves mention here (Feske 1998). The dismantling studies conducted thus far with EMDR indicate that the primary therapeutic agent operating in EMDR is brief exposure (Renfry and Spates 1994; Dyck 1993; Pitman et al. 1996a; Feske et al. 1997; Muris et al. 1998). Also, several studies (Martin 1998; Tallis and Smith 1994; Hekmat, Groth, and Rogers 1994) have shown that the eye-movement technique actually inhibits information processing, rather than enhances information processing as EMDR contends. These results tend to support the TAB-P proposition that the clinical utility of the eye-movement technique resides in its thought-stopping or suppressive properties. Ultimately, EMDR is likely to be found equivalent to other brief-exposure therapies when treating PTSD once a sufficient number of direct comparisons have been made. Unfortunately, EMDR is also likely to be found to have an unacceptably high relapse rate, as would any treatment that exclusively relies on brief exposure, once the long-term follow-up studies are actually conducted. Relapse rates are likely to be particularly high in cases of complex PTSD.

Duration of Treatment

The optimal frequency, spacing, and duration of therapy sessions for the TAB-P protocol is unclear. However, it is probably best to schedule ten to fifteen weekly sessions that last approximately one hour each over the course of three to four months when treating uncomplicated PTSD. The final two to five sessions generally should be spaced a few weeks apart. Complex PTSD or simple PTSD coupled with a severe comorbid disorder usually take longer than fifteen weekly sessions to treat. The exact duration of treatment will vary considerably depending on the treatment goals, the severity of the PTSD, the severity of the comorbid disorders, and the client's compliance with homework assignments and medication regimens. In an occasional case of simple PTSD in which it is safe to employ prolonged-exposure strategies without first employing brief-exposure strategies, the fifteen-session format can be reduced to as few as five sessions without compromising treatment outcome.

Assessment

Three things must be established before PTSD can be properly diagnosed. First, the client must exhibit the reexperiencing, hyperarousal, and avoidant symptoms that defines PTSD per *DSM-IV*. Second, the client must have experienced a stressor severe enough for it to be considered traumatic in nature. Third, the clusters of symptoms that define PTSD must have emerged after the occurrence of the traumatic stressor, not before. Although PTSD is not a particularly difficult diagnosis to make, a surprisingly large number of errors seem to have been made. Prior to 1980, PTSD was considerably underdiagnosed simply because it was not recognized as a valid diagnostic entity. However, since the publication of the third edition of the *DSM*, when PTSD was first given official recognition, it has been diagnosed with increasing regularity to the point where it may well be overdiagnosed today. Probably the most common diagnostic error now being made occurs when PTSD is diagnosed on the basis of reexperiencing, hyperarousal, and avoidant symptoms without establishing the presence of a traumatic stressor. This inevitably results in some PTSD false positives since none of the reexperiencing, hyperarousal, or avoidant symptoms that define PTSD are unique to it; the same symptom clusters can be found in several other disorders such as generalized anxiety disorder, obsessive-compulsive disorder, panic disorder, and phobias. In fact, PTSD can be readily construed as an interlocking set of several of these simpler anxiety disorders—see appendix A for more information. Probably the second most common error made in diagnosing PTSD today is to equate stressful life events such as a divorce, loss of a job, betrayal by a close friend, and so on with trauma. Certainly these types of events are highly stressful and often generate many PTSD-like symptoms, but they lack the critical element of being life-threatening in nature. Perhaps the third most common error is to mistake malingering or factitious PTSD for PTSD. Efforts should always be made to rule out these disorders in situations where monetary compensation and forensic issues are at stake, given that most psychiatric symptoms can be feigned and PTSD is now a fairly well-known psychiatric entity. The primary means of differentiating between factitious PTSD and the real thing is by way of information obtained from third parties that collaborates the client's self-report concerning the nature of his or her traumatic experiences, the absence of PTSD symptoms prior to the trauma, and the emergence of those symptoms after the trauma. Clients with factitious disorders can also be identified by their tendency to be either overly dramatic or unduly emotionally flat when describing their traumatic experiences. They also tend to have contradictions and implausibilities in their stories, and they tend to overplay popular stereotypes when relating their stories and describing their symptoms (Lanyon 1997; Rosen 1995).

Time is at a premium in most clinical settings. The clinician has an hour or two at the most to make a diagnosis, develop a treatment plan, and, most importantly, build the foundation for a collaborative and supportive therapeutic relationship. This process is best begun with a series of screening questions that address medical problems, medication, organicity, substance abuse, violence, suicide, overall level and types of psychopathology, and the nature and severity of current psychosocial stressors (see the section "Self-Rating Scales," in this introduction). The knowledge gained by these global screens enables the clinician to quickly rule out competing diagnoses and comorbid disorders that may modify or even preclude the treatment of PTSD, should PTSD be present. Once the global screens have been completed, the clients should be asked to describe their presenting problems in their own words. Should either the global screens or the clients' descriptions of the presenting problems suggest that PTSD is present, then PTSD should be more specifically addressed. This phase of the assessment can be accomplished by way of an unstructured interview or by way of one of several structured clinical interviews that have been developed for this purpose, such as the seventeen-item PTSD Symptom Scale—Interview (Foa et al. 1993) or the seventeen-item Structured Interview for PTSD (Davidson et al. 1990). Both of these instruments are psychometrically sound and take less than thirty minutes to administer. A number of practical and psychometrically sound paper-and-pencil self-report measures can also be used to bolster this aspect of the assessment process: the Posttraumatic Stress Diagnostic Scale (Foa 1996), Davidson's Trauma Scale (Davidson et al. 1998), and the Modified PTSD Symptom Scale: Self-Report Version (Falsetti et al. 1993). Please see Appendix B for a copy of the Modified PTSD Symptom Scale that you can use with your clients. Finally, the global screen for psychopathology can be augmented by way of paper-and-pencil client self-report measures such as the Symptom Checklist 90R (Derogatis 1983) or the Brief Symptom Inventory (Derogatis and Melisaratos 1983), which is an abbreviated version of the SCL-90R. The SCL-90R and the BSI both rate psychopathology across nine dimensions (somatic distress, obsessive-compulsive symptoms, interpersonal sensitivity, depression, anxiety, hostility, phobic anxiety, paranoid ideation, psychoticism), and both instruments provide three global measures of the severity of clients' psychopathology as well. Both of these instruments are very practical ones with good psychometric properties, plus the SCL-90R even has a PTSD subscale (Weathers et al. 1996; Saunders, Arata, and Kilpatrick 1990).

The process of conducting global screens before assessing a client's presenting problem may violate some client's implicit expectations for describing their presenting problem to the therapist at the outset of therapy. Usually, this problem can be readily overcome by employing a medical metaphor—likening the process to going to the emergency room with a broken leg and having the attending physician check vital signs before proceeding to set the leg.

Self-Rating Scales

Recommended self-report measures specific to PTSD include the Posttraumatic Stress Diagnostic Scale (Foa 1996), and the Modified PTSD Symptom Scale (Falsetti et al. 1993). Falsetti's Modified PTSD Symptom Scale is reproduced in Appendix B, and you can use it as a pre and post-treatment measure of PTSD symptoms. The Symptom Checklist 90-R (Derogatis 1983) and the Brief Symptom Inventory (Derogatis and Melisaratos 1983) are also recommended, because they measure overall levels and types of psychological distress in addition to PTSD. The Brief Symptom Inventory lends itself particularly well to repeated assessments of psychological distress across sessions. These measures are all psychometrically sound and quite practical. Information on how to obtain them can be found in appendix D.

The Modified PTSD Symptom Scale (see Appendix B) or the unvalidated PTSD Self-Assessment Questionnaire that follows can be used as a quick weekly measure of PTSD symptoms. First, clients will need to familiarize themselves with the subjective units of distress (SUD) scale, below. (Clients will be asked to report their levels of psychological distress—using the SUD scale—throughout the course of their treatment, particularly during their exposure work.) Finally, an unvalidated instrument that assists clinicians in screening for comorbidity is also included below, following the Self-Assessment Questionnaire.

The Subjective Units of Distress (SUD) Scale

The subjective units of distress—or SUD—scale is a convenient way of communicating to other people how much distress you are experiencing at any given time. There are eleven points on the scale, ranging from zero (absolutely complete relaxation) up to ten (extreme distress). Be sure your clients have reviewed this scale and have the ratings fixed in their minds so that when you ask them for a "SUD rating" they can quickly communicate to you their level of distress.

Rating

Zero: Complete relaxation. Deep sleep, no distress at all.

One: Awake but very relaxed; dosing off. Your mind wanders and drifts, similar to what you might feel just prior to falling asleep

Two: Relaxing at the beach, relaxing at home in front of a warm fire on a wintry day, or walking peacefully in the woods.

Three: The amount of tension and stress needed to keep your attention from wandering, to keep your head erect, and so on. This tension and stress is not experienced as unpleasant; it is "normal."

Four: Mild distress such as mild feelings of bodily tension, mild worry, mild apprehension, mild fear, or mild anxiety. Somewhat unpleasant but easily tolerated.

Five: Mild to moderate distress. Distinctly unpleasant but insufficient to produce many bodily symptoms.

Six: Moderate distress. Very unpleasant feelings of fear, anxiety, anger, worry, apprehension, and/or substantial bodily tension such as a headache or upset stomach. Distinctly unpleasant but tolerable sensations; you're still able to think clearly. What most people would describe as a "bad day," but your ability to work, drive, converse, and so on is not impeded.

Seven: Moderately high distress that makes concentration hard. Fairly intense bodily distress.

Eight: High distress. High levels of fear, anxiety, worry, apprehension, and/or bodily tension. These feelings cannot be tolerated very long. Thinking and problem-solving is impaired. Bodily distress is substantial. Ability to work, drive, converse, and so on is difficult.

Nine: High to extreme distress. Thinking is substantially impaired.

Ten: Extreme distress, panic- and terror-stricken, extreme bodily tension. The maximum amount of fear, anxiety, and/or apprehension you can possibly imagine.

PTSD Self-Assessment Questionnaire

Name: _____

Date: _____

Please rate the frequency of your symptoms in the past week (or other time period specified by your therapist). Use the SUD scale to rate the average amount of distress you experienced for each symptom.

	Frequency	**Average SUDs**
1. Number of nightmares in which you relived a traumatic event:		
2. Number of intrusive unwanted thoughts during the day about a traumatic event:		
3. Number of panic attacks:		
4. Number of times you avoided a situation, person, or an activity out of fear of a panic attack, an intrusive thought, or loss of control of your anger:		

Global Screening Questions

Name: _____

Date: _____

Ask the client to answer the following questions in a sentence or two. A possible problem should be indicated by an asterisk, and more detailed information should be gathered about the problem.

Medical Screen

Are you currently taking any medications? If so, what are they and what are they for (dosage, prescribing physician, duration)?

Are you currently being treated or evaluated for any medical problems such as asthma, high blood pressure, or diabetes? If so, what is the nature of the problem (symptoms, duration, treatment, physician)?

Current Psychosocial Stressors Screen

How would you describe your housing situation? Behind in rent? Facing eviction? Unstable in any way?

How would you describe your financial situation? Poor? Getting by? Great shape? Okay?

How would you describe your job (if appropriate)? Hate it? Love it? How are your relations with supervisors? Relations with coworkers?

How would you describe your marriage? Poor? Okay? Great?

How would you describe your children (if appropriate)? Any major problems with their physical, mental, social or educational health?

How would you describe your overall social support? Alone? Any friends, neighbors, coworkers, or family you can count on and feel close to?

Do you have any legal actions pending such as divorce, DWI, probation, bankruptcy?

Compensation/Secondary Gain Screen

Are you pursuing a compensation (such as "workman's comp") or disability claim (such as VA or SS) presently or do you expect to?

Substance Abuse Screen

Have you ever been treated for drug or alcohol abuse?

Have you ever thought you might have a problem with drugs or alcohol or has anyone you know ever suggested you might have such a problem? What has your alcohol and drug usage been like in the past thirty days?

Cognitive Screen

Do you have a lot more trouble remembering things now than before? Do you have any numbness, tingling, or loss of function in any of your arms, hands, legs, or feet?

Do you have a lot more trouble reading, writing, speaking, or doing math now than before?

Psychopathology Screen

Have you ever been treated for any kind of mental health problem such as depression on either an inpatient or outpatient basis before? If so, when, where, and what was the type of treatment?

Have you ever attempted to harm yourself in any fashion? If so, when? What were the circumstances? Did you require any medical services?

Are you considering harming yourself at the present time? If so, why? Specific plans? Any reasons why you would not harm yourself?

Have you ever lost control and physically assaulted anyone? If so, when, and what were the circumstances? Do you feel you are at risk of losing control at the present time?

Have you ever been arrested? If so, when, and what were the circumstances?

Have you had problems sleeping in the past thirty days? Any nightmares or night sweats?

Any significant weight gain or loss in past six months? How's your appetite?

How would you describe your mood in the past thirty days? Deepest, darkest depression? Okay? Happy?

Have you ever had periods in your life where you seemed to have boundless energy, didn't sleep for several days, your mind raced, you started many tasks and completed few, and you perhaps drove too fast or spent money unwisely? If so, were these episodes related to drug or alcohol usage?

Do you have any unusual fears or phobias? Any people, places, or things you go out of your way to avoid; and if you don't, you become extremely fearful or anxious? If so, what is their nature? How much do they interfere with your life?

Have you ever had a panic attack? If so, frequency, circumstances, triggers, family history? How much do they interfere with your life?

Do you have any reoccurring nightmares or highly bothersome dreams? If so, what is there nature and frequency, and do they seem to relate to any events that have taken place in your life?

Do you have any unwanted reoccurring thoughts or memories during the day that provoke high levels of distress? If so, what is their nature and frequency, and do they seem to relate to any events that have taken place in your life?

Were you ever sexually or physically abused as a child? If so, what was the nature of the abuse?

Have you ever had periods of time where you had extremely vivid dreams while awake—so vivid that you behaved as if they were real? If so, what is the nature and frequency, and could you decribe the most recent episode?

Sometimes, with prolonged sleep deprivation, prolonged stress, or while under the influence of drugs or alcohol, people see or hear things that aren't really there. Have you ever experienced anything like that? Was it caused by drug or alcohol abuse or withdrawal? Did it ever occur in the absence of drugs or alcohol?

Goals and Limitations of Treatment

PTSD treatment outcomes with the TAB-P protocol depend heavily on the type of PTSD being treated as well as on the type and severity of any comorbid disorders that may be present. Ideal or good treatment outcomes should be expected in fifteen sessions or less in 75 percent of the cases of simple PTSD that are uncomplicated by any severe comorbid disorders. Ideal treatment outcomes are defined as the permanent elimination of all PTSD symptoms, including avoidant and hyperarousal as well as reexperiencing symptoms. Good treatment outcomes are defined as the permanent and substantial reduction of the frequency and vexatiousness occasioned by the PTSD symptoms to the point that the symptoms minimally disrupt the client's vocational, interpersonal, and leisure pursuits. Ideal or good treatment outcomes can also be expected in a high percentage of the cases of simple PTSD that are complicated by less severe comorbid disorders such as other anxiety disorders or dysthymia. Treatment may take a few more than fifteen sessions, however. Complex PTSD and simple PTSD complicated by severe comorbid disorders such as a personality disorder or a long-standing substance-abuse disorder are more difficult to treat. Treatment of such cases usually takes substantially longer than fifteen sessions, and the prognosis generally is poorer. Nonetheless, good treatment outcomes can still be had with such cases provided the TAB-P protocol is coupled with a substantial amount of supportive problem-solving and medication, when needed. In some cases of complex PTSD, treatment goals need to be quite limited. For example, a realistic treatment goal might be simply to keep the client from deteriorating to the point that hospitalization becomes necessary. PTSD that is complicated by substantial secondary gain is highly refractory to treatment. Improvement is unlikely until the reinforcers that are maintaining the PTSD symptoms are removed or substantially reduced. Regardless of the specific treatment goals, it is important to negotiate them rather than impose them upon the client. Negotiating reinforces the collaborative nature of the therapeutic relationship, enhancing the chances of a positive treatment outcome.

Agenda Setting

Establishing an agenda for each session at the outset of each session is critical to effective cognitive-behavioral exposure-based treatment of PTSD. Doing so creates the highly structured format necessary for cognitive-behavioral therapy to succeed in the brief amount of time that is allotted. Each session should begin with a brief review of the overarching treatment goals, treatment strategies, and important clinical concepts. Then the results of the previous homework assignment should be reviewed, with these results being used to set the agenda for the current session. Clients who are verbose by nature may have to be frequently refocused in order to keep them on track. Of course, such refocusing efforts should always be done in a manner that preserves the supportive and collaborative nature of the therapeutic relationship. Crises that arise in a client's life sometimes require that the treatment protocol be temporarily abandoned to problem-solve the situation and work through the resulting distress. This is often the case in complex PTSD and in simple PTSD compounded by severe comorbid disorders such as a personality disorder. Balancing the need to stay on task with the need to be empathetic and sensitive to the client's ever-changing needs and concerns is a crucial therapeutic skill. Determining when and when not to break protocol is not usually easy.

Homework

Homework assignments are critical to the success of brief, cognitive-behavioral, exposure-based treatment of PTSD (see appendix C for videotapes modeling the use of homework assignments). First, homework assignments reinforce the supportive and collaborative nature of the therapeutic relationship since they are negotiated with the client, rather than dictated to the client. Second, work completed by clients on their own outside the confines of the therapy session tends to strengthen their sense of self-efficacy as treatment gains begin to be realized. And third, homework enables clients to decrease the duration of their treatment since these assignments provide them with an opportunity to greatly increase the amount of exposure work that they do over what could be accomplished within the confines of their therapy sessions. In most cases, the homework assignments should be written down as well as given verbally to the client. Clients should not be judged critically should they fail to complete a negotiated homework assignment. Instead, the reasons for the noncompliance should be explored and resolved, if possible. The therapist should always reiterate the importance of homework, however, and point out that failing to complete it will prolong treatment. Should the client prefer to utilize therapy sessions for supportive counseling and/or continually fail to comply with negotiated homework assignments, the treatment plan and treatment goals should be renegotiated and brought into line with the client's behavior.

Psychopharmacology

Simple PTSD uncomplicated by any severe comorbid disorders usually does not require the adjunctive use of medication to achieve good or ideal treatment outcomes. Nonetheless, such clients may elect to take an SSRI or tricyclic antidepressant to help them with their PTSD-related depression, sleep impairment, and panic attacks. A brief course of a benzodiazopine can also be helpful in controlling some of the PTSD-related hyperarousal symptoms. When medications are prescribed in cases of simple PTSD it is very important to emphasize that cognitive-behavioral exposure-based psychotherapy is the treatment of choice and that these medications are only being prescribed to buy some temporary relief from the more debilitating PTSD-related symptoms. Complex PTSD, on the other hand, frequently requires long-term use of adjunctive medication in the form of SSRI or tricyclic antidepressants in addition to supportive problem-solving in order to achieve good treatment outcomes. Long-term benzodiazopine use is also sometimes called for to help control PTSD-related hyperarousal symptoms and panic attacks, but much caution should be exercised with these medications because of their potential for addiction and abuse. Even neuroleptic medications are sometimes called for in cases of severe, chronic, complex PTSD in which thought disorder symptoms have developed over the course of time. For more thorough reviews of the use of adjunctive medications in the treatment of PTSD, please refer to Friedman 1988, 1991; Sutherland and Davidson 1994; Vargas and Davidson 1993.

Common Problems

The most common problem encountered when treating PTSD by way of the TAB-P protocol is what to do when comorbid disorders exist alongside the PTSD. If the comorbid disorder is in the form of a substance abuse disorder, the substance abuse should be arrested before attempting to treat the PTSD. Similarly, depression with high suicidal risk, a florid psychosis, or severe psychosocial stressors should always be addressed and stabilized first. In the case of a coexisting personality disorder, it is possible to treat the PTSD without addressing the personality disorder, but the prognosis usually is worse. The duration of such treatment is also likely to be substantially lengthened as the protocol frequently must be broken to address psychosocial stressors brought on by dysfunctional behavior related to the personality disorder. Generally, it is quite safe to conduct exposure work with personality disorder clients, even those who are quite fragile. However, a stable therapeutic alliance should be forged and strong coping effects should have accrued by way of brief imaginal-exposure work before undertaking in vivo-exposure work or imaginal prolonged-exposure work with these types of clients. In the case of other comorbid anxiety disorders, the PTSD generally should be treated first since many of these disorders are functionally related to the PTSD and will at least partially remit with the successful treatment of the PTSD. Some additional cognitive-behavioral exposure work specific to the residual comorbid anxiety disorders is usually required to completely resolve them, but such additional treatment tends to be relatively brief in duration (see appendix C for videotapes and a manual modeling the TAB-P treatment of PTSD and a comorbid panic disorder).

The second most common problem encountered when trying to treat PTSD is resistance to treatment that stems from two sources—the client and the client's primary support group. Resistance to treatment stemming from the client subsumes the concept of secondary gain and includes such things as being paid for being disabled by PTSD. A somewhat less obvious form of resistance to treatment stems from some PTSD clients' unwillingness to relinquish the victim role that often entitles them to sympathy, nurturance, and special privileges from significant others in their lives. For instance, a chronic PTSD client may be excused from some of the more odious parenting, financial management, and household maintenance tasks. The client eventually may come to assume the role of an indulged child in the household over the course of time. Along these same lines, clients can utilize their PTSD to maintain their self-esteem in the face of multiple failures and losses in their lives brought about in large part by their personality traits, substance abuse, and preexisting deficits in their social, vocational, and educational skills. PTSD may moderate some of these factors but it is seldom the exclusive or the primary cause. Such debilitated clients often assume no personal responsibility for their dysfunction, preferring instead to assume the victim role and externalize all the responsibility to their PTSD and/or to those they hold responsible for their trauma. Although this defensive strategy does serve to enhance their self-esteem, it also facilitates the adoption of a helpless, passive, and/or angry entitled stance with respect to life, thereby perpetuating the causal factors primarily responsible for their dysfunction. Resistance to PTSD treatment stemming from the client's primary social support group usually arises when the client starts to improve and begins adopting new tasks and roles vis-à-vis members of this group. Status and power issues may come to the fore as the client improves, and resentment and interpersonal conflict may ensue until a mutually acceptable homeostasis of roles is found.

Resistance to treatment is the exception rather than the rule in the treatment of PTSD. However, it is highly likely to be found when compensation is at stake, in personality-disordered clients, and in debilitated PTSD clients, such as those with severe social, vocational, and educational skills deficits. When encountered in such clients, resistance can preclude positive treatment outcomes, greatly prolong treatment, or lead to early termination from treatment. In some cases, rearranging social, psychological, and monetary reinforcers that are maintaining the client's PTSD symptoms can circumvent the resistance. In other cases, this is not feasible and PTSD treatment will have to be either abandoned all together or undertaken with the knowledge that positive treatment outcomes are unlikely. In still other cases, the personality disorder or the underlying deficits in vocational, social, and education skills might be addressed rather than the PTSD per se, but this should not be considered PTSD treatment.

Termination, Follow-Up, and Relapse Prevention

Treatment should cease once the mutually agreed-upon treatment goals have been reached. To minimize the possibility of relapse, follow-up sessions should be scheduled one month and three months after the final therapy session. The principles of cognitive-behavioral exposure-based treatment should be reviewed during these sessions, as should the clients' overall psychosocial functioning and PTSD symptoms, particularly their avoidant symptoms. Clients should be reminded that although they may have greatly reduced or eliminated their PTSD symptoms, they should not think of themselves as cured. It should be emphasized that old emotional habits die hard and could possibly return; clients should be encouraged to continue to use their newly acquired emotion-focused coping skills. The therapist should also point out that if a relapse does occur, that should not be taken as evidence that treatment failed. Instead, it should be heeded as an early wake-up call that may require the client to take a brief refresher course in cognitive-behavior therapy and again direct themselves through some brief-exposure exercises before moving on to some prolonged-exposure work. Treatment should be formally terminated in the last follow-up session, but with emphasis that the client can return if need be, that the door is always open.

Assessment and Goal Setting

Sessions 1 and 2

Objective:

The primary objective of this phase is to establish a collaborative therapeutic relationship with the client and encourage the client to view the therapist as a caring, competent, trustworthy expert capable of assisting him or her in reaching mutually agreed-upon goals. The manner in which the therapist goes about assessing and educating the client is the primary vehicle for establishing the requisite expectations and relationship.

Range of Sessions:

2 sessions are usually required.

Goals:

- Administer global screens
- Assess PTSD
- Assess expectations
- Share conclusions
- Establish treatment recommendations and goals
- Psychoeducation: assimilation work

- Psychoeducation: exposure work
- Session summary
- Feedback
- Homework—Complete one or more self-assessment tests, read selections in the accompanying client manual.

Administer Global Screens

The objective of this goal is to determine the type and severity of any problems that may be present. This is usually accomplished in the first two sessions. The conditions that should be considered include: medical problems, medications, substance abuse disorders, mood disorders, anxiety disorders, personality disorders, major mental illnesses, and a variety of psychosocial problems that include marital/family, financial, legal, health, housing, and so on. The severity of any problems that are found should be assessed, as should the likelihood that these problems will serve to complicate or even preclude treatment by way of psychotherapy. In addition, the possibility that the client will prove resistant to treatment should also be explored.

The unstructured clinical interview is the best means of obtaining the information necessary to complete this objective. A series of general open-ended questions probing each of these areas is the place to begin (the introduction provides an example of a screening questionnaire). For example, "How are things going in your marriage?" followed by more specific questions if there is any indication of problems in the area. (For example, "How often do you and your spouse argue? Has it ever gotten so bad that you separated?") Paper-and-pencil tests such as the Symptom Checklist 90R (Derogatis 1983) or the Brief Symptom Inventory (Derogatis and Melisaratos 1983), an abbreviated version of the Symptom Checklist 90R, are also very helpful in this regard. Symptoms endorsed on these scales should be followed up with general probes such as, "I noticed that you checked off that you had thoughts of ending your life on the Brief Symptom Inventory. Could you tell me a little more about that?" These general probes should be followed up with more specific questions such as, "Have you ever taken any action on these thoughts and done anything to harm yourself? When was the last time? Do you think you are in danger of harming yourself at the present time? Why not?"

The degree of possible resistance to treatment usually cannot be directly assessed. Instead, it must be inferred on the basis of a number of factors including the presence of monetary compensation or other secondary gains, the degree to which the client identifies with the role of victim, and the degree to which the PTSD is used by the client and his or her primary support group to explain/excuse dysfunctional behavior. The explanatory power afforded PTSD is usually related to the level of social, educational, and vocational skills the client has; the lower the skills the more explanatory power the client is likely to assign to the PTSD. Finally, some PTSD clients may strenuously strive to avoid any and all discussion of their trauma as well as adamantly refuse to conduct any structured exposure work, out of an unshakable conviction that such activity will only serve to make their symptoms worse.

Assess PTSD

The objective of this goal is to determine whether or not PTSD is present. This is usually accomplished in the first session or two with the criteria being those listed in the *DSM-IV*. The primary instrument that should be employed to accomplish this task is either an unstructured or a structured clinical interview such as the PTSD Symptom Scale—Interview (Foa et al. 1993) or the Structured Interview for PTSD (Davidson et al. 1990). A variety of self-report paper-and-pencil tests can also be administered to help in this assessment, such as the Davidson Trauma Scale (Davidson et al. 1998), Posttraumatic Stress Diagnostic Scale (Foa 1996), or the Modified PTSD Symptom Scale (Falsetti et al 1993), which can be found in appendix B.

Assess Expectations

The objective of this goal is to establish a good fit between the client's expectations regarding what should be done in psychotherapy, how these things should be done, what order these things should be done, by whom things should be done, and when to expect beneficial change. Usually, this is accomplished by the conclusion of the second session. In most cases, clients cannot articulate their expectations in these matters since they are at a preconscious level of awareness and/or many of their expectations are vague and ill defined. For example, some clients may expect to be "cured" or lose all their symptoms; others may not expect to invest much in their treatment in the way of completing homework assignments. If the clinician presents his or her own set of expectations on these matters to the client from a negotiating stance within the context of a collaborative relationship, then the client's implicit expectations can be made explicit and any significant differences between the two sets of expectations usually can be productively addressed.

Share Conclusions

The objective of this goal is to decide whether or not PTSD treatment should be attempted at this particular time. This is usually accomplished by the conclusion of the second session. In making this decision, both the clinician's perception and the client's perception of the client's hierarchy of clinical needs should be kept in mind. For instance, a client who is about to have his or her house foreclosed is likely to be far more concerned about housing and financial problems than about treating the PTSD symptoms. Such a severe housing/financial problem might have to be stabilized before PTSD treatment would have much chance of success. Similarly, PTSD treatment should not be initiated in the face of an active substance abuse disorder, an actively psychotic client, or a suicidal client. Treatment may be initiated in the presence of a personality disorder and substantial resistance to treatment, but it should be done with much reservation. It is preferable, of course, to have these comorbid issues successfully resolved before undertaking PTSD treatment. Generally speaking, the therapist should summarize his or her findings and conclusions and present them to the client in an informative manner toward the end of the first or second session. This should be done in such a manner as to invite the client to collaborate with the therapist in deciding whether or not PTSD treatment and/or some other treatment should be initiated.

Establish Treatment Recommendations and Goals

The objective of this goal is to establish realistic treatment goals with the client by taking into account the client's expectations, the therapist's expectations, and the clinical realities that the client is facing. Usually this goal is accomplished by the conclusion of the second session. It is generally best for the clinician to negotiate a set of treatment goals with the client from within the context of a collaborative relationship. If agreement is reached, the relationship can proceed to the treatment phase. The following is an example of how the clinician's narrative may flow in accomplishing this: "It seems that you have a number of concerns: your nightmares, your depression, and your anger and irritability. You are also having some marital problems and you are dissatisfied with your job. Your marriage is a bit troubled right now, but it appears to me to be stable and probably would improve if we were successful in reducing your irritability and your nightmares. You are also attempting to switch jobs, which seems to me to be reasonable under the circumstances, and you seem to be mounting a pretty good job search and don't appear to need any assistance there. I'm not sure exactly where to start, but I think the best place to begin would probably be to do something about your anger, your depression, and your nightmares, which all appear to be primarily related to your combat experiences. What do you think?"

If agreement is reached, refining the client's expectations of how to reach these goals and when to expect them to be reached can begin. For example, "Good, I'm glad we agree on what needs to be addressed first. My clinical experience tells me that we should be able to substantially reduce these symptoms within fifteen sessions of individual counseling on a once-a-week basis. Does that seem reasonable to you? Do you foresee any problems with coming here on a once-a-week basis?"

If agreement is reached, move on to more concretely specifying the treatment goals. For example, "Okay, good, we seem to be in agreement as to how long this treatment should take. Now let's try to be more specific about where we are headed. My clinical experience tells me that we should be able to reduce the frequency of your nightmares from four or five a week to no more than one a month and you should be able to resolve your distress upon awakening in forty-five minutes or less. Does that seem reasonable to you and is it worth working toward?"

Concepts and Skills

Psychoeducation

Assimilation Work

The objective of this goal is to insure that the client understands the treatment rationale for assimilation work. This step should normally be omitted when treating anxiety disorders other than PTSD. Usually, this goal is accomplished by the conclusion of the second session. The use of "hot memories" and "bad memories" metaphors plus the introduction of the concepts of life threat, self-ideal threat, worldview threat, and impulse threat should all be used. Clients should be introduced to these concepts through the "Traumatic-memory work" section of the client manual, reprinted below.

What Is the Purpose of Traumatic-Memory Work? The purpose of traumatic-memory work is to change memories of traumatic life events from "hot" memories to "bad" memories. Hot memories are defined as memories of traumatic events that occurred in the past and that, upon recall, elicit moderate to intense distress experienced as high levels of anxiety, fear, grief, guilt, shame, anger, and/or depression. Bad memories, on the other hand, are defined as memories of traumatic events that occurred in the past and that, upon recall, elicit unpleasant but tolerable distress in the mild to moderate range.

What Makes Hot Memories Hot? Memories are hot because the traumatic life event threatened the individual who experienced it in at least one of four ways. The event threatened the life or physical well being of the individual or other people (life threat), it threatened beliefs or expectations that the individual held about himself or herself and valued highly (self-ideal threat), it threatened assumptions or expectations about the world and the people in it that the person highly valued (worldview threat), and/or the memory arouses impulses (usually aggressive) that the individual believes will be severely punished by society if they are acted upon (impulse threat). In most cases, the memories are threatening because of a combination of life threat and one or more of the other three types of threats.

What Is Meant by Life Threat? Life threat simply refers to a serious threat to someone's life or limbs or physical harm or loss of life that actually took place. High levels of fear or anxiety would be considered normal emotional reactions to this type of threat.

What Is Meant by Self-Ideal Threat? We all have conceptions of our psychological selves, for example, one might consider oneself to be very honest, trustworthy, compassionate, intelligent, courageous, competent, or loyal, with some of these traits more highly valued than others. Sometimes traumatic life events cause us to think, feel, or behave in ways that contradict our sense of self, and when our highly valued traits are contradicted, intense distress usually results. For instance, an individual might consider himself (or herself) to be a very compassionate person and highly value that trait in himself, but later he might find himself becoming calloused and indifferent to human suffering after being hardened by combat. The memory of his indifference then could prove to be hot because the memory threatens a highly valued part of himself.

What Is Meant by Worldview Threat? We all have conceptions, assumptions, or beliefs about our world and the people who populate it that help us understand and predict what has and will occur. These expectations help us make sense of the world. Examples of such assumptions are: "There is a just and loving God," "It is a just world," "Good things happen to good people," "If you work hard you will always be rewarded," "Justice will always prevail in the end," "People are good and trustworthy," "Leaders are good, competent individuals who earned their positions and who look out for their people," "It's a safe world," "It's a predictable world," "People are basically good," and "I'm good."

Sometimes traumatic life events present us with information that contradicts some of our most cherished assumptions about the world. For instance, the death of a young child may contradict assumptions about a just world or a just and loving God. The memory of this child's death could prove to be hot because it shatters highly valued assumptions or expectations that the person had about the rules governing their world. The result would be high levels of distress upon recall of the memory.

What Is Meant by Impulse Threat? Sometimes traumatic life events arouse very strong impulses or wishes, such as strong feelings of anger or rage and intense wishes to retaliate aggressively against others. The individual may then, in turn, fear that he or she will lose control of these aggressive wishes and actually harm someone. The person may feel overwhelming guilt for having these wishes. Memories of the traumatic event become hot because the memory itself comes to elicit these dangerous aggressive wishes or impulses.

Why Don't Hot Memories and the Emotions Associated with Them Fade with Time? Actually, many traumatic memories and the intense emotions associated with them do fade over time, but not always. The most common reason for this is that the memory is not translated into words and expressed to supportive others such as friends, parents, or spouses in a safe environment. The second most common reason is that the natural curative power of dreaming about traumatic events is hindered by drugs or alcohol, and/or the emotions associated with the memory are so intense that they constantly awaken the individual from his or her sleep before the natural desensitization process of dreaming can occur. The third most common reason is that the individual does not have any self-ideals or worldviews that could make sense of the trauma and replace the old self-ideals or worldviews that were shattered by the traumatic event. Consequently, the memory doesn't make any sense, cannot be assimilated, and therefore cannot be relegated to long-term memory storage. Instead, it is stored in intermediate-term memory (temporary storage) only to repeatedly return to conscious awareness in the form of intrusive thoughts during the day and nightmares at night. The information contained in the traumatic memories is simply too important and too contradictory to the individual's view of himself or to his view of the world to be forgotten. In short, there are lessons to be learned, and the mind will not allow the memory to be transferred into long-term memory storage or be forgotten until those lessons are understood and the prevailing schemas/assumptions about one's self and one's world have been altered in such a way as to accommodate (make sense of) the discordant information contained in the traumatic memory.

Exposure Work

The objective of this goal, which usually is accomplished by the conclusion of the second session, is to insure that the client understands the treatment rationale for exposure work. Begin this process by likening PTSD to a phobia—a phobia of memories. Then explain the concepts of "conditioned" anxiety and the generalization of anxiety as well as how irrational or phobic anxiety can be resolved by way of exposure strategies. Use the "electrified chair" metaphor, below, to accomplish this. (This material is also found in the client manual.)

What Causes "Irrational" Anxiety or Phobias? Perhaps the best way to understand "irrational" anxiety is to use the fanciful notion of an electrified chair to explain how this anxiety can develop as well as explain the related concepts of conditioned anxiety and the generalization of anxiety. Suppose, for a moment, that your chair has been wired in such a way that every time you sat in it you received an electric shock. Suppose you had sat in this electrified chair one time and had received a very painful shock. What do you suppose you would think when you approached this chair the second time after receiving this very painful shock? Probably something to the effect of, "Oh, no! I'm going to get another one of those terrible shocks from that chair! It's going to hurt a lot! Maybe it will kill me!" And what do you suppose you would feel as you approached the chair and said these things to yourself? Yes, you would probably feel quite anxious and fearful. That is, your actual experience of being shocked by the chair coupled with your thoughts and expectations, or what you say to yourself as you approach the chair, both strongly contribute to how much anxiety or fear you experience in the presence of the chair. Now suppose that you have sat in the electrified chair a hundred times and have received a painful shock each and every time. What do you suppose you would be thinking or saying to yourself as you approached the chair now? Well, you would probably be saying pretty much the same thing you were saying to yourself when you approached the chair the second time, but you would likely be saying it in a shorthand fashion. For example, you might only say, "Uh, oh" to yourself, but "Uh, oh" would have the same meaning to you as the longer phrases you were uttering to yourself the first few times you approached the electrified chair. The abbreviated, shorthand messages are called automatic thoughts. What are you feeling at this time? Again, you would probably feel quite anxious and fearful not only because of your painful experiences with the chair but also because of your automatic thoughts. This type of anxiety is called conditioned anxiety.

Now, what do you suppose would happen if you approached other chairs in the room after receiving a hundred shocks in the chair and pairing these shocks with your automatic thoughts? Yes, even though you had never received any shocks in these other chairs you would probably experience a considerable amount of anxiety or fear as you approached them. This process is called the generalization of anxiety, and automatic thoughts play a big part in this process just as they did in conditioned anxiety. That is, if you think to yourself something to the effect that "these other chairs are just like the electrified chair" as you approach them you are going to experience what is called irrational anxiety, and it is highly likely that this self-talk is going to occur in the form of highly condensed, brief automatic thoughts such as, "Uh, oh." And because this self-talk is so condensed, so brief, and so automatic, it is also highly likely that you will not be consciously aware of your automatic thoughts when they occur. Thus, you can become "irrationally" afraid of many things that you have never actually been harmed by. The key to this process is automatic thoughts.

To illustrate this using another example, suppose the electrified chair in which you received all those shocks was unplugged and you knew it was impossible for you to receive another shock. What do you suppose you would feel as you approached this chair after receiving a hundred shocks from it, knowing full well that it was no longer dangerous as you could see it was unplugged? Yes, despite knowing that the chair was no longer dangerous, you would likely experience considerable anxiety or fear anyway—your anxiety or fear of the chair would now be irrational. And again, what would be causing this fear? Yes, automatic thoughts such as "Uh, oh" would likely occur as you approached the unplugged chair, and these thoughts would result in you being irrationally afraid of the chair even though you knew it was no longer dangerous.

Once a Phobia Has Developed, Can Anything Else Go Wrong? Yes, it can and frequently does. Suppose, for instance, that you had developed some conditioned anxiety to the chair, and the conditioned anxiety had generalized to other chairs by way of automatic thoughts so that now you irrationally feared all kinds of chairs and attempted to manage your anxiety by avoiding chairs all together. What do you imagine you might come to think about yourself and your world under these circumstances? Perhaps you would come to think of yourself as stupid, weak, or crazy for having such a fear, and your efforts to avoid chairs probably would greatly interfere with work, friends, family, and fun, causing you to miss out on many of the pleasant things life has to offer. You might also come to think of your future as hopeless and yourself as worthless and helpless. How do you suppose you would feel if you thought hopeless, worthless, and helpless thoughts most of the time? You would likely become depressed in addition to having a phobia. Suppose that instead of such thoughts you constantly reflected on the injustice or the unfairness of having a phobia of chairs. How do you suppose you would feel then? Probably very angry much of the time. Suppose that instead of those thoughts you frequently thought about the possibility of yourself losing control of your anger or your anxiety in the presence of other people and concluded that you would be humiliated or gravely endangered if this occurred? And what if you attempted to cope with this fear of humiliation and/or fear of violence by avoiding virtually all people? Yes, your anxiety would probably become much worse and you would probably feel depressed as well. So as you can see, sometimes feelings of depression or anger can develop as a consequence of a phobia, and sometimes additional fears can develop as well.

How Do You Treat Irrational Fears or Phobias? Suppose you had developed a phobia of the electrified chair by way of conditioned anxiety and your fear had generalized by way of automatic thoughts to chairs of all types. Suppose you decided it was high time to rid yourself of this fear since your avoidance of chairs was seriously interfering with your work and with your family. How might you go about teaching yourself that chairs aren't dangerous? By approaching chairs rather than avoiding them you would find that your fear would gradually subside—provided, of course, that you didn't receive any more shocks. This process of repetitively approaching the feared object is called exposure work. There are two basic ways of conducting exposure work. One way would be to choose a chair to approach and then force yourself to sit in it for an hour or two. Initially, you would experience very intense anxiety but by the end of an hour or two your anxiety would have subsided and your self-talk would have changed from "Uh, oh!" (which meant you perceived yourself to be in grave danger of receiving a very painful shock) to something like, "I don't particularly like this chair, but it's not dangerous; it can't hurt me. I'm safe." This type of exposure work, in which you force yourself to alter your automatic thought-mediated irrational anxiety by approaching the feared object for a lengthy period of time, is called prolonged-exposure work.

Another way you could reduce your irrational anxiety would be to gradually approach chairs for brief periods of time. For example, you might approach to within about ten feet of a chair and remain there until your anxiety had subsided and your self-talk had changed to something such as, "At least at ten feet, chairs are not dangerous. I can handle it." Then, you might approach to within about one foot of a chair and remain at this distance until your anxiety had subsided and your automatic thinking had changed. Next, you might briefly touch a chair repetitively for a second or two until your anxiety had subsided and your automatic thinking had changed. Next, you might briefly sit in a chair repetitively, and so on. This type of exposure work, in which you more gradually reduce your automatic thought-mediated irrational anxiety by approaching the feared object for relatively brief periods of time, is called brief-exposure work.

Is Prolonged-Exposure Work Better than Brief-Exposure Work at Reducing Irrational Anxiety? Yes and no. Prolonged-exposure work is more efficient and quicker than brief-exposure work at reducing excessive irrational anxiety. However, prolonged-exposure work generally creates high levels of distress at the outset of treatment, which some people are unwilling or unable to tolerate. Thus, it is often a very good idea to begin reducing irrational anxiety by starting with brief-exposure work and then moving on to the prolonged-exposure work once the individual's tolerance for exposure work has been enhanced and the individual has the confidence to proceed.

Is Exposure Work Always Done in the Real World? No. Sometimes exposure work is conducted by imagining feared situations, feared things, feared memories, and so on before actually approaching these feared objects in real life. This is called imaginal-exposure work and it can be done in the form of either prolonged-exposure work or brief-exposure work. Using the chair phobia as an example, a person might be asked to vividly imagine himself approaching and sitting in chairs until his irrational anxiety subsides and his automatic thoughts are changed before asking him to approach chairs in real life. When approaching chairs in real life, the person is said to be conducting in vivo exposure work ("in vivo" means "in real life"). Generally speaking, it is often beneficial to conduct imaginal-exposure work prior to conducting in vivo exposure work.

Is Exposure Work all That Is Needed to Reduce Irrational Anxiety? Sometimes exposure work is all that is needed, particularly when the irrational anxiety is in the form of specific phobias, that is, limited to very specific situations (such as public speaking) or to very specific objects (such as dogs) and has not generalized very much. Sometimes, however, the exposure work must be accompanied by efforts to reduce excessive emotional distress in the form of depression, guilt or shame, and/or anger that can develop along with or because of the irrational fear, such as is often seen in posttraumatic stress disorder. Efforts to reduce these other emotional reactions usually requires that the therapist help the individuals change their beliefs and self-talk with regard to themselves and their world in addition to changing their beliefs and self-talk about the object that provokes their irrational anxiety.

Session Summary

At the conclusion of each session, it is a good idea to briefly summarize what has taken place in the session. Be sure to highlight the most critical issues or points that were raised in the session. For example, at the conclusion of a session devoted to presentation of the treatment rationale, the therapist might say, "Good, it looks like you have a very good understanding of how we will be using exposure strategies and assimilation strategies to treat your PTSD."

Feedback

After summarizing the session, it is also important to ask the clients if they have any questions. This reinforces the educational endeavors that have taken place in the session and also reinforces the collaborative and supportive nature of the therapeutic relationship.

Homework

Homework for the one to two sessions in this phase usually involves completing some self-report measures to assess PTSD and/or comorbid issues as well as reading selections in the accompanying client manual. The assignments should be written down as well as given verbally to the client.

Emotion-Focused Coping-Skills Training

Sessions 3 and 4

Objective:

The primary objective of this phase is to educate the client as to the subjective units of distress (SUD) scale as well as to train the client to apply the eye-movement technique, and the relaxation response as emotion-focused coping skills.

Range of Sessions:

2 sessions are usually required.

Goals:

- Review current status
- Review homework
- Set agenda for the session
- Psychoeducation: educate as to the SUD scale
- Skill-building: train in the eye-movement technique
- Skill-building: train in compartmentalization of worry

- Skill-building: train in the relaxation response
- Session summary
- Feedback
- Homework—Rehearse coping skills

Monitoring of Current Status

The client should complete a self-assessment instrument to assess his or her overall distress as well as target symptoms at the outset of each session. The Brief Symptom Inventory (Derogatis and Melisaratos 1983) is the preferred instrument, but either the PTSD Self-Assessment Questionnaire found in the introduction or the Modified PTSD Symptom Scale in appendix B can be substituted. The client can also simply be asked, for example, "How many trauma-related nightmares did you have in the past week, and how distressing were they in terms of SUDs?"

The initial session of this phase, as well as all subsequent treatment sessions, should include a brief review of the client's overall psychosocial functioning. "Any major changes at work or at home, or are things pretty much as they have been? Any pressing concerns or issues I'm not aware of?" If a personal crisis has arisen, some of the session may need to focus on the crisis and/or the client's affective response to the crisis. For example, "Do you think we should devote some time to this problem today, or should we remain focused on what we started out to accomplish?" In most cases, the client should be encouraged to remain focused on the primary treatment goals. Occasionally, however, a serious crisis will take precedence and the PTSD treatment protocol will have to be temporarily abandoned.

Review Homework

The next task is to review the outcome of the previous homework assignment. "How did your homework go? Were you able to accomplish it all? Any unexpected problems?" If the client fails to accomplish the agreed-upon homework assignment, the reasons for this noncompliance should be explored and corrected, if possible. By asking about the homework assignment and troubleshooting any problems the client might have had with his or her homework at the beginning of each session, the importance of the homework is repeatedly underscored throughout treatment.

Agenda

The initial session of this phase, as well as all subsequent treatment sessions, should begin by your asking the client to briefly restate the treatment goals, for example, "If you and I work well together something is going to happen. What is it? What are your treatment goals? How will we know when we're done?" Then go on to briefly review the treatment strategy. "And how many sessions should this take? And how will you go about accomplishing this?"

The next step is to establish a tentative agenda for the session based on the reviews of the client's current status and homework assignment. This is normally done by briefly summarizing what has been accomplished and proposing what needs to be accomplished in the session. "Good. It looks like you had some good success this week with using the eye-movement technique to help control your distress. I'd suggest moving on to learning to use the relaxation response as an additional coping device."

Concepts and Skills

Psychoeducation

Educate as to the SUD Scale

The objective of this goal is to insure that the client understands and can apply the SUD scale (this is presented in the introduction). The scale begins at zero (absolute relaxation, no tension, deep asleep) progresses through three (normal tension, enough to keep your attention focused and head erect, but not experienced as distress), and ends at ten (extreme distress, terror-stricken, a severe panic attack). This goal is usually accomplished by the conclusion of the third session. The section in the client manual pertaining to this matter should be assigned to the client after the concept has been introduced during a session. Efforts should be made to normalize anxiety in this educational process, for example, "Anxiety and bodily tension in mild and moderate doses are normal and functional as they enable us to concentrate and keep our minds and bodies toned for action."

Skill-Building

Train in the Eye-Movement Technique

The objective of this goal is to train the client to utilize the eye-movement technique as a self-directed emotion-focused coping skill. Marquis (1991), in a series of seventy-eight case studies, reported that eleven of his clients safely and effectively utilized the eye-movement technique as a self-directed anxiety-management tool to control their excessive anxiety during in vivo exposure trials. Wolpe and Abrams (1991) also reported the successful use of the eye-movement technique as a self-directed anxiety-management technique in a case of rape-induced PTSD. I have successfully trained over 250 clients with a variety of disorders to use the eye-movement technique in this manner without any adverse treatment effects arising from it. The eye-movement technique should be introduced first because it appears to have better suppressive properties than other suppressive techniques such as thought-stopping or compartmentalization of worry and because it can be so quickly and readily taught to clients.

Basic Steps of the Eye-Movement Technique. This technique involves having the clients rapidly move their eyes from side to side at the rate of two back-and-forth movements per second. The standard dose is between twenty to thirty back-and-forth movements. When first introducing the technique (a word-for-word example is provided on the next page), the therapist should request that the client think of a moderately distressing current or past event and with their eyes open conjure up a visual image having to do with the event. The client should be encouraged to allow his or her distress to rise to between five and six SUDs (moderate distress). Generally it is best to allow the client to select the event, which does not necessarily have to be trauma related. Once the client's SUDs get into the five to six range, the therapist should direct the client through a standard dose of eye movements. This is done by asking the client to follow the therapist's finger, which is held twelve to fourteen inches in front of the client's face, while the therapist moves the finger rapidly back and forth across the client's line of vision. After this, the client should be asked if there were any changes in the image, the thoughts, or the SUDs. If there's no change, the procedure should be repeated for a second and possibly a third dose of eye movements. If changes are noted in thoughts ("I can't think about it when I move my eyes like that"), images ("The image seems more distant, less real now than before"), and/or in SUDs ("My SUDs went from about five and a half to three and a half"), then the procedure should be deemed a success and "probably helpful" for the client when suppression is likely to be needed. Next, the client should be asked to repeat this same procedure on his own with his eyes open, shifting his eyes back and forth from two appropriately spaced focal points such as the client's knees or the corners of the room. The therapist should correct any misapplication of the technique by the client at this point. Next, the process should be repeated with the client's eyes closed. The therapist should emphasize the importance of self-directed eye movements since the therapist cannot always be present when a suppressive technique is needed. The therapist should also point out the portability of the eyes-closed procedure since it can be inconspicuously employed by the client in such places as a dentist's waiting room, where the eyes-open procedure might not be appropriate if people are around. The client should be introduced to the eye-movement technique much as follows (excerpted from Smyth 1996a, 1996b; See appendix C).

An Example of the Eye-Movement Technique. Now, I'm going to show you what's called the eye-movement technique. It's about the silliest-looking thing you can imagine, but about two-thirds of the clients I have used it with seem to benefit from it and I'd like you to try it to see if it will work for you. What I'm going to do is ask you to think about a problem that is moderately upsetting—certainly no more than six SUDs. Then I'm going to put my finger in front of your face and I'm going to move it rather rapidly from side to side. What I want you to do is follow my finger with your eyes without moving your head. If this procedure works for you, you should notice a decrease in your SUDs level, your thoughts about the problem should be blocked, or images related to the problem should be altered in some fashion. Now, I can't guarantee that you will benefit from this procedure, but it certainly seems worth a try. Again, all I want you to do is follow my finger with your eyes as I move it back and forth while you are thinking about a problem. Okay? Any questions? Good, let's begin. What's your SUDs level right now? In a moment I want you to start thinking about a problem that should kick you up to six SUDs or so. Got that problem in mind? Begin stewing, thinking about it, and depict the problem or an aspect of the problem in your mind's eye. Okay, thinking about it? Got an image of it? Good, now follow my finger keeping your head as still as possible. (A dose of eye-movements follows.) Now that was the standard dose of eye movements, about thirty back-and-forth movements. Did you notice any change in your SUDs, your thoughts, or the images? (If no change, repeat. If change noted, proceed). Good, it looks like this procedure might well benefit you. Now, I want you to do this on your own and demonstrate to both of us that you know how to apply it. That is, I want you to purposely think about the problem again, switch on an image having to do with the problem, and allow your SUDs to get to about six or so. But this time, I want you to direct yourself through the eye movements using the corners of the room or your knees to focus on rather than my finger. Any questions? Good. Okay, on your own, switch on thoughts and images of the problem. Got it? Where are your SUDs? Now calm yourself down using the eye movements. (A dose of eye movements follows. If successful, then move on to the eyes-closed procedure). Good, it looks like the eye-movement technique is going to be of some value to you. Now, I'd like you to try this same experiment with your eyes closed. Obviously, it might be inappropriate to use the eye-movement technique with your eyes open in some social situations. But even in these types of situations, you can still use it by closing your eyes and then shielding them with your hand as if you are deep in thought. Just like this. (The therapist models the procedure.) It will also prove very useful in the imaginal-exposure work that we are likely to be doing. So go ahead. Close your eyes, conjure up a problem, get a good clear visual image of it, think about it, worry about it, stew about it, and push yourself to five to six SUDs. Then with your eyes closed, I'd like you to move your eyes rapidly back and forth about twenty-five or thirty times. Okay, go ahead, close your eyes, conjure up a problem, and let me know when you are in the five to six range.

Train in Compartmentalization of Worry

The compartmentalization-of-worry technique should not be routinely introduced to all PTSD clients. Instead it should be reserved for those PTSD clients with comorbid generalized anxiety disorders who chronically and excessively ruminate about a variety of problems in their lives. In the compartmentalization-of-worry procedure, clients are paradoxically directed by the therapist to worry at specific times and in specific places in an effort to get their ruminations under better stimulus control. For example, a client might be directed to think and worry about his or her mother's health for an hour between nine and ten each morning while sitting in the living room and to steadfastly refuse to think about the matter at other times or in other places. This procedure can be used by itself or in combination with the eye-movement technique. For example, a client might use the self-directed eye-movement technique when he first notices himself beginning to think about his mother's health to suppress the thoughts coupled with the words, "Not now, later" and then proceed to worry for an hour between nine and ten the next day.

Train in the Relaxation Response

The objective of this goal is to train the client to induce the relaxation response and to apply it as an anxiety-prevention technique as well as an anxiety-management technique (see appendix C for a videotape and manual). Usually, training in the relaxation response is begun by the fourth session and its application continues throughout treatment. The basic steps in applied-relaxation training are:

1. The therapist should direct the client through a twenty- to twenty-five minute relaxation exercise using a combination of relaxation techniques, including progressive muscle relaxation, passive muscle relaxation, slow rhythmic breathing, and positive mental imagery. Proper breathing should be emphasized. The exercise should be recorded and the recording given to the client.

2. The client should practice the relaxation response a few times by way of the tape recording, and then he or she should practice inducing the relaxation response without the aid of the tape. The client should conduct at least five self-directed relaxation exercises as homework each week, more if he or she is willing.

3. The client should practice applying the relaxation response in the context of imaginal and in vivo brief-exposure exercises in-session, and later as homework. He or she should also practice utilizing the relaxation response as preparation for known stressors in-session, and later as homework. Throughout treatment, the client should be encouraged to use the relaxation response as an in vivo coping skill whenever the need arises, as well as simply a form of meditation.

The client should be introduced to applied-relaxation training by the therapist's paraphrasing the following section in the client manual.

Tips for Relaxation Training. At one time early in our lives, we all probably knew how to relax, but gradually, many of us lose this ability as we grow older, become more and more achievement-oriented, and begin to abuse stimulants such as caffeine and nicotine. Our innate ability to calm ourselves down, to rest, to relax, becomes increasingly difficult in a highly competitive world that encourages and rewards achievement and aggression. Certainly hard work, striving to get ahead, and industriousness are all laudable traits, but sometimes they can be overdone. Our work ethic can and does go awry from time to time, which can lead to chronic and excessive stress and possible somatic symptoms such as headaches and ulcers. As the old saying goes, there can be too much of a good thing.

Cognitive-behavioral therapy incorporates what is called relaxation training in an effort to help people restore a healthy balance between their achievement strivings and their need to relax, rest, and replenish themselves. More specifically, relaxation training is designed to teach people how to induce the relaxation or quieting response so that they can keep themselves reasonably calm in competitive (for example, test-taking) situations. The relaxation response can be learned in ways other than through relaxation training: yoga, transcendental meditation, autogenic training, hypnosis, biofeedback therapy, and some forms of physical exercise. The main advantages of relaxation training are: it is simpler to learn and takes less time than some of the other approaches, it is not couched in Eastern mysticism, and it can be applied in virtually any situation that a person might encounter.

Main points to keep in mind as you induce the relaxation response:

- There is no right way or wrong way to induce the relaxation response.
  You will be introduced to a variety of procedures designed to induce the relaxation response, including progressive muscle relaxation, passive muscle relaxation, breathing exercises, and directed visual imagery. Your task is to try them all, experiment a bit, and come up with the procedure(s) that works the best for you.

- The relaxation response is a learned skill and like any learned skill it requires practice.
  With practice, you will find that the relaxation response becomes easier and quicker to induce, and you will become more adept at inducing it in more and more difficult situations. With sufficient practice, you should be able to induce the relaxation response in a matter of a minute or two. Sometimes it can be induced in a matter of seconds.

- Make it easy on yourself.
  When you first start out learning to induce the relaxation response, you should be reasonably comfortable when you begin; don't attempt to induce it if you are highly distressed until you have developed sufficient skill to handle high levels of stress.

- Understand that it does not always work.
  Like any learned skill, sometimes you will be "on" and you will be able to quickly and easily induce the relaxation response. Other times you will be "off" and will not be able to relax yourself very quickly, easily, or deeply. Practice does improve one's ability to induce the relaxation response, but there will still be times when the response will not come as easily as you would like.

- Make it fun.
  Although you do need to practice, don't overdo it. In most cases, you will need to induce the relaxation response a minimum of five times a week. There is no maximum, but stop when you feel that it is getting boring or bothersome.

- Intrusive thoughts should be expected.
  You are likely to have bothersome, distracting thoughts come to mind that will momentarily capture your attention and increase your stress while you are inducing the relaxation response. That's to be expected. Probably the best

way to handle them is to simply allow them to pass in and then pass out of your mind without devoting much attention to them or damning yourself for having them. With practice, intrusive thoughts are less likely to occur and will become less intrusive.

- Your relaxation response does not have to be perfect to be beneficial. Although some people are able to achieve profound levels of mental and physical relaxation, not everyone will be able to do so, and you don't have to reach extremely deep levels of relaxation to experience the benefits. Becoming adept at inducing mild to moderate degrees of relaxation is usually sufficient to accomplish what most people want to accomplish in cognitive-behavioral therapy.

- Breathing properly is very important in inducing the relaxation response. People often take many rapid, shallow breaths when frightened—this is called hyperventilation. Hyperventilation, however, actually can create anxious feelings in your body by putting too much oxygen in your blood. Probably the best way to prevent hyperventilation is to take a normal breath and then force yourself to exhale slowly by saying "R-e-e-e-e-l-a-a-x-x-x" slowly and gently to yourself two or three times before taking the next breath. This will slow down your breathing and prevent the hyperventilation-induced feelings of anxiety from occurring.

- If you have chronic and excessive high levels of stress, you need to practice the relaxation response at least once a day (preferably twice) on a regular basis.
  If you are innately high-strung, you will have to integrate the relaxation response into your daily life. Otherwise the gains you make from relaxation training are likely to be short-lived.

So I'm Relaxed, Now What? There are a number of different ways that you can put the relaxation response to use once you have mastered it. Four of the most common ways are as follows:

1. It can be used as a form of meditation.
   Many people find that practicing the relaxation response once or twice a day on a regular basis can be very helpful in reducing the incidence of chronic stress-related symptoms such as headaches, gastritis, and so on. Ten or fifteen minutes once or twice a day is usually all the time that is needed, but it must be induced on a regular basis for the benefits to be maintained.

2. It can be used to reduce insomnia.
   Inducing the relaxation response in bed as a way of preparing oneself for sleep often proves useful in reducing restlessness and sleeplessness. Again, this requires it to be practiced on a fairly regular basis.

3. It can be used to control stress in certain stressful situations such as test-taking, public speaking, or job interviewing.
   The relaxation response can be used to prevent the arousal of excessive stress in many situations if the individual practices prior to entering the

stressful situation. For example, arriving at a prospective employer's office twenty minutes early and self-inducing the relaxation response while you wait to meet him or her can be very helpful in keeping down the stress you do experience during the interview.

It also can be used to reduce the stress you experience while you are actually in the stressful situation. For example, you might take a minute or two to self-induce the relaxation response by means of an abbreviated relaxation exercise while you are in the process of taking an important exam, if you begin to notice that your stress is becoming uncomfortably high.

4. It can be used in conjunction with anxiety-management training to eliminate or greatly reduce simple phobias, social phobias, and chronic performance anxiety.

Examples include fear of flying, severe test anxiety, and excessive fear of making a social error. Anxiety-management training is a procedure in which the person becomes relaxed, vividly imagines stressful scenes, and then is taught to use the relaxation response and what is called "rational" self-talk to calm himself or herself down and remain calm while vividly imagining stressful situations. Once the person can control stress in imagined situations, he is gradually introduced to the same situation in real life, where again he is taught to control his stress through the use of the relaxation response and rational self-talk.

The following excerpt from Smyth (1998a, 1998b; see appendix C) is an example of how relaxation training was applied in the treatment of a case of complex combat-induced PTSD.

Therapist: Today I'd like to begin the relaxation training that we talked about last week and you read about in your client manual. What I hope to do is train you to induce the relaxation response by way of what I call the smorgasbord approach. In this approach, I'm going to use a variety of techniques, including what is called the progressive muscle relaxation technique in which I'm going to ask you to briefly tense a number of different muscles in your body before relaxing them. I'm also going to be using the passive muscle relaxation technique in which I ask you to go back over the same muscles you tensed earlier and relax them again but without first tensing them. I'm also going to ask you to use your imagination to calm yourself by imagining yourself in a peaceful, safe, and relaxing place. I like to imagine myself at a quiet beach on a warm summer day. Some people like to imagine themselves on a walk through the woods on a peaceful autumn day, or curled up inside in front of a crackling fire on a snowy, wintry day. How about you? What type of scene do you think you would find relaxing?

Client: The beach sounds good. I think a walk in the woods might remind me of Vietnam.

Therapist: Good, the beach it is, then. One other very important relaxation technique that I'm going to show you is the slow breathing technique. Very simply, I'm going to ask you to concentrate on your breathing and be sure to breathe slowly and regularly—saying the word "relax" two or three times between each breath. In this way, you will be able to slow down your breathing and prevent what is called hyperventilation, which is shallow and rapid breathing that causes people to feel even more anxious and experience a variety of unpleasant bodily sensations such as light-headedness, tingling sensations, and the like. Okay? Any questions?

Client: No, I did some of this before and I remember it helped some.

Therapist: Good. Where are your SUDs right now, before we begin the relaxation training?

Client: Oh, about five or five and a half.

Therapist: Good, you should be able to reduce your SUDs to maybe the three to four range. If you were at six or above, it might not work very well. Usually it takes some practice before the relaxation response can be used to reduce distress in the six-plus range. Okay, let's begin. I'd like you to place both feet flat on the floor and get as comfortable as you can in the chair. I'd also like you to close your eyes and begin focusing your attention on my voice. I'm going to record this relaxation training exercise, if it's all right with you. I'm going to give the tape recording to you afterward, and I'd like you to use it as a guide in some homework that I'd like you to do. Okay?

Client: Okay.

Therapist: Go ahead and close your eyes, settle back into the chair with both feet flat on the floor, and focus your attention on my voice.

The therapist begins tape recording the relaxation training exercise at this point.

Therapist: I'd like you to begin by focusing your attention on your breathing. I'd like you take a normal breath, hold it briefly, and now exhale slowly, gently—saying "relax . . . relax" two or three times silently to yourself between each and every breath. Air in, and now out, slowly, saying "relax . . . relax" silently to yourself two or three times between each and every breath. Slowly and gently now. Normal breath, and now exhale gently and slowly, saying "relax" two or three times between each and every breath. Not only does breathing slowly and gently help you relax, it prevents hyperventilation, which can make your distress a lot worse. Good. Air in, and now out slowly and gently. Relax . . . relax.

Now I'd like you to focus on the muscles in your right foot and leg. Think about those muscles for a moment. I'd like you to briefly tense those muscles up by pushing down against the floor with the heel of your right foot. Go ahead, push down with the heel of your right foot and feel the tension that you produced in the muscles of your right foot, right calf, and right upper leg. Tense, tense, tense. Now let go, relax those same muscles that you were tensing up in your right foot and leg, and feel the difference between tension and relaxation. Okay, good.

Now think about the muscles in your left foot and leg. I'd like you to tense those muscles up by pushing down against the floor with the heel of your left foot. Feel the tension, now, in the muscles of your left foot, your left calf, and your left upper leg. Tense, tense, tense. Now relax. Let the tension fade away; let the muscles relax in your left foot, left calf, left upper leg. More and more relaxed now, and feel the difference between the tension that you produced in those muscles a minute ago and the feelings of relaxation as you relax further and further. More and more relaxed now.

Now focus your attention on the muscles in your stomach. I'd like you to tense those muscles up just as if you were going to do a sit-up. Tense, tense, tense. Now relax those same muscles in your stomach and feel the difference between tension and relaxation. More and more relaxed now. Stomach muscles more and more relaxed.

And now shift your attention to the muscles in your right hand and arm. Purposely tense them up by making a fist with your right hand and squeeze it tightly. Feel the tension now in the fingers of your right hand, your wrist and forearm, and your right upper arm. Tense, tense, tense, and now relax. Let the tension fade away as you relax the muscles in your right hand, right wrist and forearm, and right upper arm. More and more relaxed; and again notice the difference between tension that you produced a minute ago and the feelings of relaxation in your right hand and arm.

Now your left hand and arm. Think about them for a minute, and purposely tense those muscles up by making a fist with your left hand and squeeze it tightly. Tense, tense, tense, and now relax those same muscles. Feel the difference between the tension you produced and the feeling of relaxation in your left hand, left wrist and forearm, left upper arm. More and more relaxed, now; more and more relaxed.

Now think about the muscles in your neck and shoulders. I'd like you to purposely tense those muscles up by shrugging your shoulders up and forward and holding them there. Shrug your shoulders up and forward, hold them there for a moment, and feel the tension in those neck and shoulder muscles. And now let them relax, relax, and feel the difference between tension and relaxation in your neck and shoulder muscles. More and more relaxed now; peaceful and calm, very, very relaxed.

Now shift your attention to the muscles in your forehead. I'd like you to tense your forehead muscles by frowning or furrowing your brow, and hold it. Feel the tension in those forehead muscles. Tense, tense, tense, and now relax. Let all the tension in those forehead muscles fade away, fade away. More and more relaxed, more and more relaxed, now. Make your forehead as smooth as a pane of glass, and notice the difference between tension and relaxation. Your forehead as smooth as a pane of glass, now. More and more relaxed. More and more relaxed. Peaceful and calm, and very, very relaxed.

And now the muscles around your eyes. Briefly tense these muscles up by squinting your eyes tightly shut. Feel the tension now, tense,

tense. And now relax, let those muscles around your eyes go limp and relaxed. More and more relaxed now; more and more relaxed, peaceful, and calm.

And now your jaw muscles, tense them up by clenching your teeth tightly together. Tense, tense, tense, and now relax. Let the tension fade away, and feel the difference between tension that you produced a minute ago and feelings of relaxation as you relax those muscles in your jaw more and more. More and more relaxed now; peaceful and calm, all the tension fading away.

And now the muscles around your mouth. I'd like you to think about them for a moment and purposely tense them up by pressing your lips tightly shut. Purse your lips tightly together, and feel the tension. Tense, tense, tense, and now relax. Let the tension in those muscles about your mouth become more and more relaxed, peaceful, and calm. Very, very relaxed now; peaceful and calm.

And now I'd like you to check your breathing again to make sure that you are breathing slowly and gently. Taking the air in, and then letting the air out slowly, pacing your exhalation with two or three "relaxes" between each and every breath. Air in, and now out, slowly, gently, relax, relax, relax. Two or three "relaxes" between each and every breath.

And now I'd like you to go back over those same muscles groups and make sure they are peacefully and calmly relaxed. If you notice any tension has crept back into the muscles, just take a minute and let it go. Usually, you should be able to do this by simply directing the muscles to relax, but occasionally, you may have to briefly tense the muscle once again before relaxing it. Okay, check the muscles in your right foot, right calf, and right upper leg. Make sure they are peaceful, calm, and relaxed. If any tension has developed, just let it go. Right foot, right calf, right upper leg, more and more relaxed, peaceful, and calm. And now your left foot and leg, check them to make sure they are peaceful, calm, and relaxed. Left foot, left calf, and left upper leg. More and more relaxed, peaceful, and calm. And now your stomach muscles, check them, make sure they are peaceful, calm, and relaxed. If any tension has developed, just let it go. More and more relaxed now. Very, very relaxed, peaceful and calm. And now check your right hand and arm, make sure they are peaceful, calm, and relaxed. Right hand, forearm, upper arm, more and more relaxed now. And now your left hand and arm, check those muscles to make sure they are peaceful, calm, and relaxed. More and more relaxed. If any tension is noticed in any of these muscles, just let it go. Let it fade away. And now the muscles in your neck and shoulders, check them, make sure they are limp and relaxed. Peaceful and calm, more and more relaxed. And now your forehead, make sure it's as smooth as a pane of glass, smooth as a pane of glass, very, very relaxed, peaceful and calm. And now the muscles around your eyes, check them and make sure they are limp and relaxed, peaceful and calm, very, very relaxed. And now your jaw muscles, check them. Make sure your jaw muscles are limp and relaxed, peaceful and calm. And now the muscles around your mouth, check them. Make sure they are peaceful, calm, and very, very relaxed. And now, once again, check your breathing. Breathing gently and slowly, taking the air in and then letting it out slowly. Two or three "relaxes" between each and every breath. Air in, and now out slowly, gently, relax, relax, relax.

And now I'd like you to use your imagination to help you relax even further. I'd like you to imagine yourself on a beach somewhere on a warm, lazy summer day. It might be a beach you have actually visited before, or it might be one that you are imagining for the first time. In any event, it's a beautiful beach; the sun is shining, and the waves are lapping onto the beach. I'd like you to notice the beach, the grayish white sand that seems to stretch on forever. It's a beautiful beach; you might notice some seashells or stones washed smooth by the surf there on the beach if you look closely. Notice the water, the waves, as they gently lap onto the beach, gently ebbing and flowing. And notice the water, the bluish green water, how beautiful it is and how the sun dances, sparkles as it is reflected off the water. So peaceful and calm. And notice the sky, the blue, blue sky dotted by puffy white clouds here and there. And feel the warmth of the sun as it warms your hands, your arms, and your face. Just feel that warm summer sun warming your face and hands, refreshing and relaxing you more and more. You might even notice a gentle sea breeze, wafting in off the water and gently rustling your hair. You can almost taste the saltiness in the air. So peaceful and calm, and very, very relaxing. I'd like you to leave the beach for now and let your mind go blank. Once again, I'd like you to check your breathing since breathing is so important to relaxing. Just check to make sure that you are taking a normal breath, holding it briefly, and then exhaling gently and slowly, pacing that exhalation with two or three "relaxes" between each and every breath. Air in, and now out slowly, gently, relax, relax, relax.

Okay, that concludes the relaxation training exercise. In a moment now I'd like you to open your eyes once again, but remain as peaceful and calm as you possibly can. And remember, the relaxation response is a learned skill and it takes some practice to master it, but with some practice you should be able to use it to help manage your excessive distress. Also remember that there is no right or wrong way to induce the relaxation response, just use whatever works best for you. Try out all the various relaxation techniques that I have introduced you to today, but don't be afraid to experiment a bit and come up with a combination that works best for you. The one technique that I do emphasize with everyone, however, is the controlled, slow breathing. So please keep that no matter what else you choose to keep or discard. With practice, you should find that you will be able to induce the relaxation response under more and more trying conditions and you should be able to induce it very quickly—perhaps as short as a minute or so. But this requires practice and rehearsal. Okay, go ahead, open your eyes, but keep yourself as peacefully relaxed as possible.

The client opens his eyes at this point and the tape recorder is shut off.

Session Summary

At the conclusion of each session, summarize the main points of critical issues that surfaced in the course of the session.

Feedback

After summarizing a session—and especially after negotiating a homework assignment with the client—it is always important to ask if he or she has any questions. This not only reinforces the educational endeavors that were conducted in the session, but also underscores the collaborative nature of the therapeutic relationship.

Homework

Homework for this phase involves educating the client as to the SUD scale (presented in the introduction) and the two emotion-focused coping skills. A typical homework assignment for a week might entail five relaxation exercises and five in vivo attempts to apply coping skills. The assignments should be written down as well as given verbally to the client. They are listed below in their preferred order of occurrence.

1. Experiment with the eye-movement technique. Try it out at least five times to see if you can use it as an emotion-focused coping device when you notice your distress getting into the five to six SUDs range.

2. Practice inducing the relaxation response at least five times this week as a form of meditation.

3. Experiment with the relaxation response this week. Try it out at least three times this week to see if you can use it as an emotion-focused coping device when you find yourself getting into the five to six SUDs range. Also try it as preparation for encountering a known stressor at least two or three times this week.

4. Experiment with combining the eye-movement technique, and the relaxation response as emotion-focused coping devices at least five times this week when you first notice that your distress is getting into the five to six SUDs range.

Phase III

Assimilation Work

Session 5

Objective:

The objective of this phase is to review the traumatic memories in their entirety and reduce the associated emotional distress by using assimilation and rational thinking strategies. Straightforward didactic explanations, Socratic questioning, and the use of metaphors are the primary therapeutic tools used to accomplish this. During the reviews, clients must be able to keep their distress at six and a half SUDs or below by way of rational thinking alone in order to benefit. Many PTSD clients cannot meet this criteria, in which case this phase should be passed over in favor of the next phase of treatment—the brief-exposure work phase. Occasionally, however, clients with simple PTSD of recent origin that is not complicated by other disorders can be successfully treated using only assimilation and rational thinking strategies, without the need for brief-exposure or prolonged-exposure strategies. This tends to occur when the predominant form of emotional distress elicited by trauma-related stimuli is something other than anxiety such as guilt, shame, grief or anger.

Range of Sessions:

1–9 sessions required, depending on the complexity of the PTSD.

Goals:

- Review current status
- Review homework
- Set agenda for the session
- Psychoeducation: rational thinking
- Psychoeducation: assimilation work
- Psychoeducation: using metaphors and expressions
- Skill-building: the basic principles of assimilation
- Session summary
- Feedback
- Homework—Review recorded memories with assimilation strategies

Monitoring of Current Status

All sessions in this phase should have a brief review, near the outset of each session, of the client's overall psychosocial functioning: "Is everything continuing to go okay at work and at home?" Should a serious crisis have arisen, some supportive problem-solving may be required before continuing with the PTSD treatment. Questions should also be asked about the prevalence and vexatiousness of the client's PTSD and related symptoms in the previous week. This can also be accomplished by administering a self-assessment instrument such as the questionnaire in the introduction or the Modified PTSD Symptom Scale found in appendix B. This will create the expectation that some therapeutic gains will soon begin to be realized, and it will monitor treatment progress.

Review Homework

The next task is to review the outcome of the previous homework assignment, which usually involves repetitive reviews of the traumatic memories utilizing only assimilation and rational thinking strategies to manage the ensuing distress. Special attention should be paid to the number of reviews that the client conducted as well as the degree of distress that was elicited by the reviews. Expectations for the development of coping and desensitization effects should be created in the process. For example, "Did you notice any difference in the amount of distress provoked, or the ease with which you managed the distress that was provoked, when you compare the first time you reviewed the memory with the last time you reviewed it?" The reasons for any noncompliance with the homework assignment should be explored and corrected, if possible. Usually, several important clinical concepts are reviewed in the process, such as the SUD scale and the rationale for exposure and assimilation work.

Agenda

The sessions in this phase should begin by asking the client to restate the overarching treatment goals: "What is it you're trying to accomplish here, and how long should it take?" Again, set the agenda for the sessions in this phase based on what was found in the reviews of the client's current status and homework assignment. For example, "Good. You got five reviews in this week and noticed that the memory bothered you much less the last time you reviewed it when compared to the first time. That's the desensitization effect we were looking for. I'd like to go over the memory again in here today, but this time I'm going to spend a lot more time on the 'hot spot.' Would you mind if I record it again, just in case it proves useful in structuring your next homework assignment?"

Concepts and Skills

Psychoeducation

Train in Rational Thinking

The objective of this goal is to train the client to utilize rational thinking as an emotion-focused coping skill (see appendix C for videotapes and a manual). This is accomplished by educating the client as to the importance of cognitive appraisals and the beliefs or assumptions that underlie these appraisals in preparation for the assimilation phase of treatment, where efforts will be made to modify some of the client's irrational automatic thoughts and associated beliefs. A brief review of these concepts is usually all that is needed since the concepts of irrational anxiety, irrational beliefs, generalization of anxiety, and automatic thoughts have all been introduced earlier by way of the "Electrified Chair" and "Traumatic Memory Work" readings and metaphors. In this review, automatic thoughts should be characterized as brief, terse thoughts and images that the client almost automatically employs to make sense of events in his or her life. Automatic thoughts should also be characterized as usually occurring at a preconscious level of awareness, and when properly decoded, automatic thoughts should be characterized as reflecting some of the assumptions, beliefs, or expectations that the client is operating under. Finally, the client should be made aware of the fact that some automatic thoughts are irrational and contribute to excessive distress because they greatly exaggerate the threat posed by events, and/or they discredit or discount positive events, and/or they misattribute fault or blame. Make sure the client has read the following sections in the client manual: "Rational Thinking and the ABC Model," "Five Common Irrational Beliefs," "Five Common Distortions in Thinking," and "Correcting Irrational Self-Talk."

Psychoeducation

Assimilation Work

Reviews of the clients' traumatic memories occupy the majority of the time in each of the sessions in this phase. During the reviews, Socratic questioning and metaphors are used to help the clients assimilate the discordant information found in their traumatic memories. These assimilation strategies have much in common with the rational-thinking strategies popularized by Ellis (1975) and Beck (1976). Both rational-thinking strategies and assimilation strategies attempt to alter conscious or preconscious cognitive appraisals that engender clients' excessive emotional distress. Both types of strategies assume the presence of underlying assumptions, beliefs, or schema that clients use to understand their world and themselves, and both types of strategies utilize many of the same therapeutic tactics to accomplish their objectives, such as Socratic questioning and straightforward didactic endeavors. The primary difference between assimilation strategies and rational-thinking strategies is that assimilation strategies target more of the clients' deeper or overarching beliefs about themselves and their world than do rational-thinking strategies (Mahoney 1993; Robins and Hayes 1993; Meichenbaum 1993). Assimilation strategies also tend to utilize metaphors to a greater extent than do rational-thinking strategies. As a consequence, assimilation strategies have a more intellectual or philosophical appearance. For example, rational-thinking strategies might be used to address the peripheral belief that, "If someone rejects me, I am less of a person"; whereas assimilation strategies might be used to address the underlying core beliefs of, "I am unlovable" or "I am bad" (Robins and Hayes 1993).

Assimilation strategies frequently play a crucial role in the treatment of PTSD, particularly complex PTSD, but they generally play a much smaller role in the treatment of most of the other anxiety disorders. In PTSD, clients are usually being presented with information in their traumatic memories that is incongruent with the schema or assumptions that they have used to make sense of their past and present experiences, for example, killing a wounded friend while in combat in order to spare him from a torturous death. Because of this incongruency, the traumatic memory remains "stuck" in intermediate or active memory and in a nonvolitional manner enters conscious awareness periodically in the form of intrusive thoughts and nightmares until the incongruency is resolved (Smyth 1994a; Epstein 1994; Horowitz 1986). Resolution of the incongruency is best achieved by first accessing the "stuck" memory and then having the client use secondary-process thinking to examine the contradictions contained therein in light of assimilation strategies introduced by the therapist.

In this process, the therapist gently but firmly guides the client toward viewing his or her tragedy in a personally and socially healthy manner. This allows the client to resolve the discrepancies between his beliefs about himself and his world that are contradicted by the information contained in his traumatic memories (Kubany and Manke 1995; Resick 1993). For example, "No matter what I did it was going to be wrong. It was a damned-if-you-do-and-damned-if-you-don't type of situation. Killing my friend was the best I could do under the circumstances. If the roles had been reversed, I would have wanted my friend to kill me to keep me from falling into the hands of the enemy, and thereby sparing me the misery of an agonizing death. It was really an act of kindness, and it was really about the only thing I could do for my friend under the circumstances."

Exposure work often must be conducted prior to any assimilation work being done to reduce the intensity of the distress elicited by the clients' traumatic memories. This is required since assimilation strategies are heavily dependent on secondary-process thinking, which is thought to become ineffectual for most clients at high levels of physiological arousal (see appendix A). In short, it is impossible to cognitively reframe events in the midst of a panic attack. Regardless of which assimilation strategy is used, it is thought to be maximized when the therapist employs as little inducement as is necessary to get the client to try out these alternative therapeutic beliefs (Smyth 1994a). This is a well-established principle of attitude-change procedures (Strong 1978).

The incongruent information found in PTSD clients' traumatic memories usually contradicts beliefs the clients hold about the world being a just, orderly, predictable, and safe place, and/or their memories contradict their beliefs about the existence of a just and loving God. Their memories may also contradict their beliefs about themselves or others being good, competent, valued, worthwhile human beings (Smyth 1994a, 1994b). The primary therapeutic task becomes identifying the nature of the contradictions or incongruencies and then finding a way to resolve the resulting cognitive dissonance. This can be accomplished by either changing the cognitive appraisals of the clients' traumatic experiences and memories and/or by changing the schema that the trauma-related data contradicts (Smyth 1994a; Meichenbaum 1994; Horowitz 1986). This data-assimilation task is best accomplished by the therapist using a straightforward didactic method coupled with Socratic questioning.

Socratic Questioning. In Socratic questioning, the therapist asks the client a series of leading questions designed to identify and correct the inconsistencies and contradictions contained in the client's appraisals of the traumatic experiences. Expressions that have assimilation strategies embedded in them are also very helpful in this regard (Smyth 1994a; Meichenbaum 1994). For example, in the case of "just world" contradictions, the following expressions have been found to be of use: "It rains on the just as well as the unjust," "Shit happens," and "Bad things happen to good people." In the case of "good self" or "good others" contradictions, the following expressions have been found to be of use: "To err is human," "Damned if you do and damned if you don't," "Caught between the devil and the deep blue sea," and "Let he who is without sin cast the first stone." In the case of intense anger and retaliatory wishes that are impairing recovery, the following expressions have been found to be of some use: "Legitimate but unproductive anger," "The sweetest revenge is to live life well," and "Better dig two graves if you intend to bury your enemy."

The assimilation process is begun by first activating the traumatic memory and bringing it into conscious awareness where the memory, or the assumption it contradicts, can be modified by way of the secondary-process thinking program. After activation of the traumatic memory and with physiological arousal in the moderate range, the therapist then should begin probing the inferred incongruencies by way of a series of Socratic questions designed to bring the usually preconscious contradictions into conscious awareness. As noted above, this usually involves asking the client a series of leading questions that serves to undermine the irrational appraisals associated with the traumatic memories, as well as highlight and/or exaggerate the irrational nature of the client's appraisals.

For example, in response to excessive guilt and irrational attributions of responsibility for being "greedy" and accepting an invitation to get an ice cream cone that led to a client being molested at ten years of age, a therapist might query, "Well, I guess that makes you a brazen greedy hussy who ought to burn in hell, doesn't it?" This query is followed by, "What's wrong with this statement?" as well as, "How do you suppose I would look at this?" In another example, a client with combat-induced PTSD who had witnessed the death of forty soldiers had misattributed their deaths to himself in the form of thoughts to the effect that, "If only I had done my job better, they wouldn't have died." He was gently probed with the following series of questions: "Did you fire the missile that killed them? Did you fire the rocket that intercepted the enemy's missile, causing it to break apart and fall where it did? Did you design or construct the unreinforced barracks that housed those soldiers? Could you or should you have known the missile was going to fall where it did? Suppose you had trained them better, suppose you had trained them to be perfect soldiers, would that have changed anything? Why not? Ever hear of friendly fire? How often do you think that friendly fire is responsible for deaths of fellow soldiers in war situations? Is it possible that friendly fire killed those men, or was it the enemy's missile, or was it both of these things that killed those men? Did your sergeant, who knew you and the circumstances, hold you responsible for their deaths? Why not? How about your commanding officer? Why not? And how do you think I might view this? Do you think I would hold you responsible for their deaths? Why not?" Next, the irrational appraisal is usually stated in a somewhat exaggerated form: "So, if I were to say to you that you were grossly negligent, your negligence caused forty young men to die, and you are guilty of murder, what would you say to me? What's wrong with that statement?"

Once the client can articulate a rational, less pathogenic explanation, the therapist should recapitulate it in an abbreviated form: "So, you're telling me that their deaths were caused by friendly fire, not by your negligence, and that you did a reasonable job under the circumstances. Is that correct? How believable does that seem to you right now?" If the client reports that it doesn't seem credible, proceed with further Socratic questioning to identify any residual irrational appraisals. Once the rational thinking seems at least somewhat credible to the clients, proceed to point out to them that although their rational mind now understands, they still need to re-educate the irrational automatic-thinking portion of their mind, which can only be done through repetition.

Listed below are some questions that clients can be asked by the therapist. The clients can also use the questions on their own to help them correct or dispute irrational appraisals that they have identified.

1. What evidence do you have to support this thought?

2. Is there any alternative way of looking at the situation or yourself?

3. Is there any alternative explanation?

4. How do you think I, your therapist, would view this situation? How would (valued person) think of it?

5. Are you caught up in "should-have"s and "must-have"s?

6. What's the worst possible outcome?

7. How long will this unpleasant situation last?

8. On the grand scale of injustice or badness, how unjust or bad is it?

9. Are you confusing a remote possibility with a high probability outcome?

10. Are you overestimating the amount of responsibility you have for the situation?

11. Are you discounting/discrediting positive aspects of the situation or your ability?

Using Metaphors and Expressions

Words, phrases, or stories can all serve as useful metaphors to facilitate the assimilation process by suggesting alternative, more mentally healthy ways of appraising trauma-related experiences. Metaphors should be introduced to clients at appropriate times after activation of their traumatic memories and should be presented in general terms that are followed by efforts to get the clients to apply the assimilation strategy embedded within the metaphor to themselves and to their traumatic experiences. For example, a client who is attributing excessive blame to himself and is trying to undo the tragedy with a lot of "what if I had . . ." type of thinking could be asked, "Have you ever heard the expression, 'closing the barn door after the horse is out'? What does it mean? Have you ever done any barn-door closing after the horse was out in your life? When? Ever observe anyone else do it? When? How might this be applied here with respect to the death of your friend?"

Ideally, the therapist should tailor his or her expressions and stories to the needs of each client individually, for example, sports and military metaphors for people interested in those things, religious metaphors for the devoutly religious, and so on. However, it is usually more practical to have a set of general metaphors that the therapist is comfortable with and that are culturally acceptable and well understood by the clinical population with whom the therapist is working. The set should include metaphors that facilitate the assimilation of data encoded in traumatic memories that contradict each of the following assumptions: a just and orderly world, a good self, good others, and a safe world. What follows is a set of metaphors that I have found useful in my work with combat-induced PTSD. It is offered for illustrative purposes only and should not be considered exhaustive for combat-induced PTSD nor particularly useful for other clinical populations.

Metaphors. "The beast" is a useful metaphor for assimilating memories of rage-driven brutality and atrocities, and intense, homicidal, sadistic aggressive wishes that clients have observed in themselves or in others that challenge their "good self" or "good other" assumptions. It can be introduced in the following fashion: "The beast wins wars, the beast survives, and it has been developed by eons of evolution (or by God). The beast serves the interests of self-preservation and the preservation of the species, for it often arises when loved ones' lives are threatened. The beast may be the darker side of human nature, but it is a part of human nature nonetheless. It's very much a part of every human being walking the face of this earth. Most people don't know of the beast since war or other traumatic events are needed to bring it to the fore. Although it's a part of human nature, it is not the essence of human nature. The beast and Mother Teresa exist side by side in each of us. You and I know of the beast and of the conditions that call it forth. You and I also know how dangerous it can be. It's important not to damn ourselves for having the beast, but it's also important that we put it back in its cage where it belongs until we need it again, such as when our lives or our loved ones' lives are actually being threatened. Can you see any value in the beast? Can you see any good in the beast? Can you be a good, worthwhile person and have known the beast on a personal basis? How is that possible? Do you think I would condemn you for having the beast visit you? Why not?"

"The torturer" is a useful metaphor for assimilating memories of torturous behavior and calloused indifference to human suffering that clients have observed in themselves or others that challenge their "good self" or "good others" assumptions. It can be introduced in the following fashion: "You and I may not like it, but the torturer is very much a part of human nature, part of our heritage developed by eons of evolution (or God). It may be the darker side of human nature, but it is a part of human nature nonetheless. Can you see how becoming calloused and indifferent to human suffering was adaptive—necessary for your survival in a war zone? Yes, that's right, if you had allowed yourself to feel and see the enemy as a fellow human being you not only would have endangered yourself but others in your platoon. What then were your options? Continue to feel and care and endanger yourself and your fellow soldiers, or become hardened, calloused, and indifferent in order to survive? Was it a reasonable choice to become hardened and numb under the circumstances? It was another damned-if-you-do-and-damned-if-you-don't situation, wasn't it? Have you ever heard of a psychologist by the name of Milgram? Let me tell you about his studies on obedience and compliance and how easy he found it to induce college students to torture other college students. [Proceed to describe Milgram's experiments here. A useful bibliotherapy tool is "The Education of a Torturer," by Gibson and Haritos-Fatouros, 1986.] So it would appear that given the right conditions, most any human being can be induced to torture others, doesn't it? Military training and the social conditions of war would certainly seem to me to be the type of conditions that would likely bring the torturer to the foreground, don't you think? So is it possible for you to be a worthwhile human being even though you had the torturer with you? How so? Is it possible for human beings to be good even though all of us can become torturers? How so? What do you suppose we have to do to keep the torturer at bay? Yes, when law and order break down, as they do under war conditions, the torturer and the beast are likely to emerge. By keeping ourselves attached to others and by keeping our social institutions strong such as our families, schools, courts, and police, we can prevent the conditions from arising that bring the torturer to the fore."

"Damned if you do and damned if you don't" is a useful expression for assimilating memories in which the client or others made a calculated decision that knowingly resulted in tragic consequences and that challenged "good self," "good other," or "just world" assumptions. "Have you ever been confronted with a situation in which you were going to be wrong no matter what you did? Tell me about it. Yes, life constantly presents us with damned-if-you-do-and-damned-if-you-don't situations. I'm sure you had some prior to war and I'm sure you've had some since you returned. The difference, of course, is that in war they were life-and-death decisions. No matter what you did you were going to be wrong and somebody was going to die. There were no right answers, were there? Only two wrong ones to choose from. You had a choice to make and you had only seconds to make it. Was your decision a reasonable one under the circumstances? Well, was it? Remember, there were only two wrong answers to choose from. Did you make a reasonable one? What do you think I think about your decision? Do you think I would feel it was a reasonable one? Why? Perhaps you've been asking yourself the wrong question here. Perhaps you have been asking yourself if you made the right decision. But there was no right decision, only two wrong ones. Again, was your choice a reasonable one under the circumstances? Is it possible for people to make decisions that cost other people their lives and still be good, worthwhile human beings? Well, is it? How can that be? Yes, that's exactly right. Sometimes life presents us with damned-if-you-do-and-damned-if-you-don't situations. How long and how much should you be punished for making a reasonable decision under those circumstances? Perhaps you've punished yourself enough."

"Shit happens" is a useful expression for assimilating clients' memories that challenge their "just and orderly world" assumptions. It can be introduced in the following fashion: "You keep asking, 'why did it happen?' Probably you will never know for certain. Have you ever known bad things to happen to good people before? Yes, and I know that we all want to believe that if we 'do good' and are 'good' that this somehow protects us from such things. But does it? [Use examples of bad things happening to good people that are pertinent and appropriate for the client, such as, "How about Jesus Christ? He did good and was good and look what happened to Him."] Perhaps it is best to think of life as basically fair and just, but sometimes things will go wrong—very wrong—through no fault of our own despite all our good efforts. Perhaps it is more reasonable to think that we don't live in a perfectly just world but only a reasonably just world. Sometimes random buckets of shit will be dumped upon us no matter what we do. Most of these buckets will be on the smallish side, but occasionally there will be big buckets, like right now. No one is immune; everybody has a few random buckets of shit visited upon them during the course of their lifetime. Sometimes shit happens. Is it possible to go on, survive, even thrive in a reasonably just world rather than a perfectly just world? Have you ever known anyone who has had a major bucket of shit dropped on him and recovered? Tell me about him. Yes, he recovered and so will you."

Skill-Building

The Basic Principles of Assimilation

The basic principles of applying assimilation strategies in the treatment of PTSD are as follows (see appendix C for videotapes and manuals):

1. Access the clients' traumatic memories while keeping their physiological arousal in the mild to moderate range. Sometimes this requires that some brief-exposure work be conducted before beginning the assimilation work, particularly when a client is readily overwhelmed with affective arousal upon even the most transient access to their traumatic memories.

2. Introduce a metaphor or use personal or professional anecdotes that have assimilation strategies embedded within them that provide the clients with a means of accommodating the discordant information contained in their traumatic memories.

3. Use Socratic questioning to induce the clients to view their tragedy from this new and accommodating point of view—or simply ask the clients to try out this viewpoint from some other valued person's point of view, such as the therapist's. This process frequently involves slightly exaggerating the irrational aspects of the clients' prevailing and nonaccommodating point of view, and then inducing the clients to correct or dispute the irrational aspects.

4. Have the clients rehearse viewing their traumatic experiences from the vantage point of their new accommodating point of view while also rehearsing disputes to the irrational aspects of their old nonaccommodating point of view. This rehearsal should initially be done in the therapist's presence, but it can and should be tape-recorded for use by the clients in their homework assignments. This type of rehearsal generally should be done in a prolonged-exposure format in which clients think about and imagine their traumatic experiences in the form of a story or narrative. This can also be accomplished by writing about the tragedy.

An Example of Assimilation Work. Following is an example of how assimilation work was accomplished using Socratic questioning and metaphors in the treatment of a case of simple combat-induced PTSD. (Excerpted from Smyth 1998c; 1998d; see appendix C.)

The client had recounted his Persian Gulf war experiences in a more or less chronological fashion in the presence of the therapist in a previous session, and two "hot spots" had been identified—one dealing with his homicidal intentions toward his commanding officer (CO) and the other being when he had observed grotesque enemy dead at close range.

Therapist: Okay, I'd like you to go back to that part of your memory when you were in the same tank as your CO and just before the land assault began. You were riding behind your company's tanks, which were getting in line to begin the assault. You were thinking that your CO was incompetent, mentally unstable, tactically inept, and that he was going to get a lot of the men killed, although your unit had only suffered a few minor injuries thus far. Got that part of your memory in your mind's eye? Can you still picture it?

Client: Yes, the visual memory is still very vivid. I can see the desert like it was yesterday.

Therapist	SUDs?
Client:	Oh, they're back up to about five and a half.
Therapist:	And why had you come to think this about your friend and CO? What had you observed that made you think that he was incompetent and was going to get a lot of men killed?
Client:	He would confide in me about how afraid he was. He couldn't sleep, and when he did fall asleep, he would wake up screaming. This was before the land assault started. He would be trembling half the time when he was awake. The first sergeant and myself tried to keep this from the men. They were frightened enough already and they certainly didn't need to see their commanding officer like this. They didn't have a whole lot of respect for him to begin with since he was so indecisive and lacked a command presence. He was so scatterbrained that you would tell him something one minute, and he would have forgotten it the next minute. He wasn't particularly tactically sound to begin with, but with no sleep and his fear being as high as it was, he simply couldn't think straight. He was almost relieved of his command early on. He must have done or said something that made Battalion HQ concerned because they sent someone out to take a look at the CO and us. Neither the first sergeant nor I said anything at the time, but I know I, for one, was hoping they would relieve him. But they didn't.
Therapist:	And why didn't you say something at the time? Why didn't you tell battalion of your concerns?
Client:	Well, this was early on. I thought he would improve, at least I was hoping he would. Besides, he was my friend, and it would have devastated him emotionally and would have ruined his career to be relieved of his command.
Therapist:	Kind of a damned-if-you-do-and-damned-if-you-don't type of situation that we talked about before, don't you think?
Client:	Yea, if I tell them what I'm thinking, then I betray a friend and undermine a superior officer. If I don't, then I may be putting a lot of young men's lives at risk.
Therapist:	Yes, that seems to be the essence of the damned-if-you-do-and-damned-if-you-don't conflict. And when you are placed in such situations, there are no right answers, just two wrong answers to choose from. You either betray a friend or possibly put some men's lives at risk. So the best you can hope for is to make a reasonable choice under these circumstances. And what was your choice?
Client:	I remained silent.
Therapist:	And was that a reasonable choice under the circumstances?
Client:	I don't know. I'm not sure.

Therapist: Remember, now, there are no right answers—just two wrong answers to choose from. Given the information you had at the time, did you make a reasonable decision? Remember, you're not God. You can't foretell the future with certainty. Given what you knew at the time, you acted in a way that sustained, rather than undermined, the chain of command, and you honored your friendship. Certainly good values to have and sustain, don't you think?

Client: Yes.

Therapist: These values of loyalty to superiors and friends are encouraged by the military, aren't they? They're good soldierly values, are they not?

Client: Yes.

Therapist: And you behaved in a fashion that upheld these important and worthwhile values, did you not?

Client: Yes.

Therapist: And you decided not to betray your friend and superior also because you thought he might just have the "pregame jitters" and would overcome them once the "game" got underway, didn't you?

Client: Yes, that's what I thought, or hoped for, anyway.

Therapist: Is that an unreasonable belief? I mean, have you known anyone to do that kind of thing before? Be an emotional wreck before the "game" starts, and then calm down once it gets underway and perform well?

Client: Yes, I've known a lot of people like that. I'm that way sometimes myself.

Therapist: So, is there any way you could have known that your CO wasn't going to settle down but was going to get worse? Remember, now, no Monday morning quarterbacking. Given the information you had at the time, did you make a reasonable decision under the circumstances?

Client: Yes, I guess I did.

Therapist: No guessing now. I'm certain you made a reasonable decision under the circumstances. Not the perfect or right decision, since there is never a perfect or right decision to be made in damned-if-you-do-and-damned-if-you-don't situations—just two wrong answers to choose from. So did you make a reasonable decision under the circumstances?

Client: Yes, it was a reasonable decision under the circumstances.

Therapist: And what about the other two men—your first sergeant and the major from your battalion? They essentially made the same decision as you did. Were they or are they bad men and bad soldiers for deciding, as you did, to leave your friend and CO in command?

Client: No, not really. They did the best they could.

Therapist: So maybe you've been asking yourself the wrong question all this time. Perhaps you've been asking yourself whether or not you made the right decision under the circumstances, when there was no right answer to be made. There were just two wrong ones to choose from. And given the two wrong answers you had to choose from, did you make a reasonable choice under the circumstances?

Client: Yes, the choice to say nothing was a reasonable one to make under the circumstances.

Therapist: SUDs?

Client: Oh, about five.

Therapist: So if I were to be your "irrational" side and state that, "You failed to make the right decision. You are incompetent, and you are a bad soldier, or a bad friend, or both," what would be a more rational or reasonable way to look at this situation? I mean was there a right answer to be found?

Client: No, it was, as you would call it, a damned-if-you-do-and-damned-if-you-don't type of situation; no matter what I chose to do, I was going to be wrong.

Therapist: Yes, but you failed to make a reasonable choice of the two wrongs, so you are a bad soldier, a bad friend, or both. What's wrong with that statement?

Client: Well, I did make a reasonable choice under the circumstances. There's no way that I could have known that my CO was going to get worse, but he certainly did.

Therapist: So you had two wrongs to choose from, and you made a reasonable choice of the two under the circumstances. But doesn't that still make you a bad soldier, a bad person, or both? Shouldn't you have known that your CO was going to get worse? What's wrong with that statement?

Client: Well, no, I couldn't predict the future with certainty. No one can. I did the best I could under the circumstances, just like the first sergeant and the major, and I respect both of them.

Therapist: And what about me? I know the circumstances; why is it that I don't condemn you and judge you to be a bad soldier or a bad person?

Client: Well, you've been in similar circumstances yourself. You've been in damned-if-you-do-and-damned-if-you-don't life-threatening circumstances yourself; you know what it is like to have to choose between two wrong answers.

Therapist: True. And that's one thing about war—many soldiers get placed in damned-if-you-do-and-damned-if-you-don't types of situations and have to choose between two bad, wrong, life-threatening alternatives. For example, the medic I was telling you about who had two seriously wounded men to attend to—by attending to one man he more or less insured that the other would die. Did he make a bad decision? Is he a bad person and a bad soldier for having made such a choice?

Client: No, all you can hope for is to make a reasonable decision under the circumstances.

Therapist: SUDs?

Client: They're down some, four and a half.

Therapist: And how is the medic's situation like yours?

Client: Well, both he and I were in damned-if-you-do-and-damned-if-you-don't types of situations. Both of us had to make decisions about who was going to live and who was going to die. I mean, I only thought I was going to have to choose between my friend and my men. I didn't actually have to act on my thoughts. I came awfully close, though. The medic had to actually act on his thoughts.

Therapist: So, having been in a damned-if-you-do-and-damned-if-you-don't life-threatening set of circumstances and forced to make a choice between two wrongs, can any good come from it? I mean is there any value in having gone through what you've gone through?

Client: I'm not sure what you mean.

Therapist: Well, my own damned-if-you-do-and-damned-if-you-don't life-threatening experiences have sensitized me and given me a lot of empathy for others who have gone through similar experiences, which is something that I certainly value. Also, I frequently use my experiences as reference points to examine contemporary problems I'm encountering. And I can assure you, whenever I ask myself, "How bad is it, really?" I always come back with, "It's nothing. It's a piece of cake" when compared to my damned-if-you-do-and-damned-if-you-don't life-threatening experiences. They kind of help me keep everything in perspective. Can you see any way of finding any value in your experiences?

Client: Well, my combat experiences certainly give me an appreciation of life and an appreciation of what being a soldier is all about—something that I doubt the average citizen has. And, yes, I probably could use some of my combat experiences as reference points to help me keep the hassles of civilian life in perspective. I certainly need that right now with all the problems at work. And I think combat has strengthened me, toughened me up. I mean, if I can get through that I can handle most obstacles that I will encounter in civilian life.

Therapist: There's also a positive in the fact that the war ended quickly. Thus you never had to act on your intentions, plus your unit suffered minimal casualties.

Client: Yes that's true. I, we, were fortunate in that regard.

Therapist: SUDs?

Client: About four SUDs now.

Therapist: Good, tell me a little more about how your combat experiences have strengthened you in some ways.

The therapist went on to review the same damned-if-you-do-and-damned-if-you-don't conflict with regard to the client's homicidal intentions toward his CO, which intensified as the war progressed. The sessions were recorded and given to the client to replay as structured assimilation-exposure homework assignments that he completed between sessions.

Session Summary

At the conclusion of each session, summarize the main points of critical issues that surfaced in the course of the session.

Feedback

After summarizing a session—and especially after negotiating a homework assignment with the client—it is always important to ask if he or she has any questions. This not only reinforces the educational endeavors that were conducted in the session, but also underscores the collaborative nature of the therapeutic relationship.

Homework

Homework for the one to nine sessions in this phase involves applying the coping skills learned in therapy while repeatedly reviewing the traumatic memory. Reviews can also take the form of written descriptions of the traumatic experience. A typical weekly assignment involves inducing the relaxation response five times as a form of meditation, reviewing the tape-recorded memory five times, and applying the emotion-focused coping skills five times in vivo. The assignments should be written down as well as given verbally to the client. The assignments for this phase are listed below in their preferred order of occurrence.

1. Continue to practice inducing the relaxation response as a form of meditation daily.

2. Continue to use the combination of the eye-movement technique, the relaxation response, and rational thinking as emotion-focused coping devices this week whenever your distress is inadvertently triggered by trauma-related environmental stimuli or you have a reexperiencing symptom. Try to employ these coping devices before you get beyond six or six and a half SUDs.

3. Listen to the tape recording we made of your traumatic memory at least five times this week, and be sure to keep your SUDs at six or below while conducting the review. Also be sure to use the rational thinking you developed in here during the review.

4. Write out a description of the traumatic event, including the thoughts and feelings you had at the time it was occurring, and then review your story five times this week. Be sure to emphasize the rational thinking you have developed in here. Also be sure to keep your distress at six SUDs or below in the process. (Optional)

Brief Exposure and Assimilation Work

Sessions 6 to 11

Objective:

The objective of this phase is to utilize brief exposure exercises to reduce the clients' emotional reactivity to the traumatic memory and related stimuli, such as somatic sensations that provoke panic and/or environmental stimuli that provoke phobic-like reactions. Strong coping effects and moderate desensitization effects should be in evidence before moving on to Phase V.

Range of Sessions:

6 or sometimes fewer sessions are usually required, depending on the complexity of the PTSD.

Goals:

- Review target symptoms and treatment goals
- Review current status
- Review homework
- Set agenda for the session

- Psychoeducation: brief-exposure work
- Skill-building: the basic principles of brief exposure
- Session summary
- Feedback
- Homework—Imaginal/in vivo brief exposure

Monitoring of Current Status

Again, review the client's overall psychosocial functioning near the outset of each of the sessions in this phase. Should a serious crisis have arisen, some supportive problem-solving may be required before continuing with the PTSD treatment. Questions should be asked about the prevalence and vexatiousness of the client's PTSD and related symptoms in the previous week. This can also be accomplished by administering a self-assessment instrument such as the Brief Symptom Inventory (Derogatis and Melisaratos 1983), the questionnaire in the introduction, or the Modified PTSD Symptom Scale found in appendix B. This creates the expectation that some therapeutic gains will soon begin to be realized, and it also monitors treatment progress.

Review Homework

Again, review the results of the client's previous homework assignment near the outset of each of the sessions in this phase. Normally, these homework assignments involve inducing the relaxation response as a form of meditation, utilizing their newly acquired emotion-focused coping skills to cope with distress arising from encounters with trauma-related stimuli, and conducting brief exposure exercises targeting trauma-related stimuli. Special attention should be paid to the amount of exposure work that the client did on his or her own as well as on the proficiency with which he or she accomplished the exposure work. Expectations for the development of coping and desensitization effects should be created in the process. For example, "Do you notice any difference in the amount of distress provoked, or the ease with which you managed the distress that was provoked, when you compare your first exposure trial to your last exposure trial?" The reasons for any noncompliance with the homework assignment should be examined and corrected, if possible. Usually, several important clinical concepts are reviewed in the process, such as the SUD scale, the CAP principle, coping effects, and desensitization effects.

Agenda

Again, the sessions in this phase should begin by asking the client to restate the overarching treatment goals: "What is it you are trying to accomplish here and how long should it take?" Again, set the agenda for sessions in this phase based on what was found in the reviews of the client's current status and homework assignments. Normally, the agenda will include a brief-exposure exercise (below).

Concepts and Skills

Psychoeducation

Brief-Exposure Work

In this phase, the majority of each session is taken up with a brief-exposure exercise. Typically, the exposure exercises begin with imaginal brief exposures to subsets of the client's feared traumatic memory and then proceed to imaginal brief-exposure exercises to related environmental stimuli. Normally, the exercises are tape recorded and used to structure the client's subsequent homework assignment.

In the anxiety disorders, it is very important to remember that clients are reacting with irrational or excessive anxiety to a complex set of feared stimuli. For example, a client with PTSD experienced excessive emotional distress whenever he encountered external visual and auditory stimuli that were associated with his traumatic experience of having been confined as a POW in a railroad boxcar that was strafed and bombed by friendly aircraft. Stimuli such as confined spaces or crowded conditions triggered the replaying of his traumatic memory, which in turn triggered a number of automatic thoughts to the effect that he was going to die, or have a panic attack and be humiliated. These automatic thoughts, in turn, triggered a number of somatic sensations including feelings of suffocation and chest pressure. These sensations in turn triggered more catastrophic automatic thoughts and images. Stating that this client was excessively fearful of confined spaces oversimplifies the problem since it was the combination of these stimuli that provoked the irrational anxiety. Confined spaces simply were a frequent starting point in a series of rapidly unfolding cognitive events that ultimately led to excessive levels of anxiety and avoidance or escape from the environmental stimuli. As is commonly the case in PTSD, this client's traumatic memories resurfaced periodically in the form of reexperiencing symptoms (nightmares and intrusive thoughts) even in the absence of any associated environmental stimuli with the same results.

The relative importance of these various components of the feared stimulus complex will vary from one person to another and from one type of anxiety disorder to another. For example, trauma-related visual imagery almost always plays a substantial role in provoking excessive anxiety in cases of PTSD, whereas somatic sensations generally play a smaller role. In cases of panic disorder, however, somatic sensations and catastrophic automatic thoughts are usually the primary causal agents of the excessive anxiety, with trauma-related imagery playing little or no role.

The basic therapeutic task in treating all anxiety disorders by way of cognitive-behavioral exposure techniques is to induce the anxiety-disordered clients to approach their feared stimulus complex in the absence of any real threat, prohibit escape from the feared stimulus complex, and reduce the ensuing distress through the passage of time and through cognitive coping strategies. The two different types of exposure strategies differ considerably in their structure of the exposure trials that accomplish this task, however. Prolonged-exposure strategies (Foa et al. 1993), which subsume such techniques as implosion (Stampf and Levis 1967) and flooding (Keane et al. 1985; Keane et al. 1989; Pitman et al. 1996b), strive to expose the clients to the entire feared stimulus complex for a prolonged period of time at the outset. Prolonged exposure strategies strive to maximize the level of distress provoked at the outset; they emphasize the therapeutic value of the passage of time while paying relatively little attention to cognitive coping strategies. Brief-exposure strategies, on the other hand, expose the client to a subset of the feared stimulus complex for a relatively brief period of time at the outset; they provoke only a moderate amount of distress during the exposure trials. Brief-exposure strategies also emphasize gradually approaching the entire feared stimulus complex over the course of a series of exposure trials, and they emphasize the importance of cognitive coping strategies to reduce the anxiety that is provoked, rather than emphasize the importance of the passage of time. Wolpe's (1958) systematic desensitization procedure is perhaps the best known of the brief-exposure strategies, and it should be considered the grandfather of all such strategies. Williams' (1990) guided mastery treatment for phobics is a contemporary brief-exposure strategy with substantial empirical support attesting to its efficacy. Meichenbaum's (1985) stress-inoculation training, as well as Suinn's (1990) anxiety-management training, can also be classified as brief-exposure strategies; both of these psychotherapies have substantial empirical evidence attesting to their efficacy in the treatment of a number of the anxiety disorders. Eye-movement desensitization and reprocessing (EMDR) can also be so classified (Shapiro 1989; Shapiro 1995; Smyth 1994a). EMDR involves repetitive brief exposures to feared imaginal stimuli followed by efforts to reduce the moderate level of distress that ensues by way of a combination of cognitive coping strategies that include rational thinking, the relaxation response, and the eye-movement technique, an image-and-thought-suppressing technique.

There are two desired outcomes in both types of exposure work—desensitization effects and coping effects. Desensitization effects are defined as the reduction in a client's distress upon exposure to feared stimuli after one or more exposure trials, with this reduction being experienced as nonvolitional on the part of the client. Coping effects, on the other hand, are defined as an increase in the ease and quickness with which clients can calm themselves down using anxiety-management techniques following one or more exposure trials in which the clients have practiced applying these techniques. This type of anxiety reduction is experienced as volitional on the part of the client. These two effects are thought to be under the control of different variables, with prolonged-exposure strategies generally producing stronger desensitization effects than brief-exposure strategies, and brief-exposure strategies generally producing stronger coping effects than prolonged-exposure strategies. Thus, it is not uncommon for anxiety-disordered clients to develop strong coping effects, but only moderate desensitization effects, following a number of brief-exposure trials. Such outcomes enable clients to manage the residual "conditioned" anxiety when confronting their feared stimuli without resorting to escape or avoidance strategies, and the clients appear to be much improved. However, the residual "conditioned" anxiety coupled with the clients' escape/avoidance tendencies are thought to predispose some clients to relapse once their formal treatment has ended (Fava et al. 1995; Fava, Grandi, and Canestrari 1991; Thase, Simons, and

McGeary 1992). Thus it behooves the therapist to further reduce this residual "conditioned" anxiety by way of prolonged-exposure strategies before terminating the active treatment phase (Smyth 1994a; Deblinger and Heflin 1996). In this way, the probable superior desensitization properties of prolonged exposure can be utilized without incurring the adverse treatment outcomes too often driven by prolonged-exposure strategies and without unduly prolonging the length of treatment. These results are achieved by eliminating the noxious agent in prolonged-exposure strategies thought to be primarily responsible for generating adverse treatment outcomes—namely the clients' perceptions of being overwhelmed by the high levels of psychological pain typically precipitated by untitrated prolonged-exposure strategies. Such high levels of distress are thought to undermine the relatively fragile therapeutic alliance in some anxiety-disordered clients, particularly those with chronic complex PTSD (Courtois 1988; Smyth 1994a). It is worth noting that the risk of adverse treatment outcomes is probably heightened when severe comorbid disorders are present and untitrated prolonged-exposure strategies are employed. The risks are also probably heightened when shame, guilt, and/or anger play large roles in the distress that is elicited when clients confront their feared stimuli (Courtois 1988; Pitman et al. 1996a; Pitman et al. 1996b). It would seem unwise, at the very best, to continue to advocate the use of untitrated prolonged exposure in the treatment of PTSD in light of the cautionary notes sounded by numerous clinicians and the mounting empirical evidence validating their concerns (Littrell 1998).

Skill-Building

The Basic Principles of Brief Exposure

The basic principles of brief exposure are as follows.

1. Anxiety-disordered clients should be trained in several cognitive coping devices to reduce and manage their distress during the ensuing exposure trials. At the very least, this should include training in rational thinking, the relaxation response, and the eye-movement technique.

2. The clients' brief-exposure work should begin with imaginal brief exposure to a clinically meaningful subset of the stimuli that define their feared stimulus complex that is capable of eliciting moderate amounts of distress, perhaps five to six SUDs. Clients should be encouraged to strive to produce five to six SUDs in each exposure trial, and then they should be encouraged to employ their emotion-focused coping skills to calm themselves back down to about four SUDs before moving on to the next exposure trial. Usually, about five exposure trials are conducted in an hour-long therapy session. The exposure exercise generally should be recorded on audiotape, which should be given to the clients to help them structure their subsequent homework assignment.

3. The duration of the clients' brief-exposure trials should be brief at the outset, usually lasting but a few minutes.

4. The duration of the clients' brief exposure trials should be increased, more and more of their feared stimulus complex should be presented, and the trials should move from imaginal exposure to in vivo exposure as desensitization and coping effects become evident.

5. The anxiety-disordered clients should be strongly encouraged to conduct exposure trials on their own outside of the therapy sessions.

6. The transition from imaginal brief exposure to a selected subset of the clients' feared stimulus complex to in vivo prolonged exposure to their entire feared stimulus complex should be guided by the CAP principle. That is, the clients should be encouraged to move on to the next step in the exposure sequence when they can no longer readily provoke five to six SUDs at the current step in the sequence. The "C" stands for "challenge, but never overwhelm yourself," in other words, clients should be encouraged to push themselves to five to six SUDs, but no more than that. The "A" stands for "apply anxiety-management techniques to reduce the distress once you've challenged yourself, never resort to escape to do so." In other words, clients should be encouraged to employ rational thinking, the relaxation response, and the eye-movement technique to cope with the distress that they have provoked in their exposure trials. The "P" stands for "practice, practice, practice." Clients should be informed that there is no substitute for repetitive exposure trials and that they should continue their exposure work until there is evidence of strong desensitization effects and coping effects. This process has a great deal in common with that advocated by Williams (1990; Williams and Zane 1997) in his guided mastery approach to treating phobics.

7. Hierarchies should be used to control the clients' affective arousal. Hierarchy construction should not be an exhaustive undertaking reminiscent of Wolpe's (1958) procedures, however. Instead, the clients should simply be asked to classify their traumatic memories and related somatic and environmental stimuli in terms of their potential to elicit distress. Brief-exposure work should begin with stimuli that are likely to provoke distress in the five to six SUDs range. Stimuli higher in the hierarchy should be addressed after coping and desensitization effects have accrued for stimuli lower in the hierarchy.

An Example of Brief-Exposure Work. The following excerpt from Smyth (1998e; 1998f; see appendix C) is an example of how brief-exposure work was conducted in the treatment of a case of simple violence-induced PTSD (a woman who had been shot).

The client had directed herself through an abbreviated relaxation exercise, which had been augmented by the therapist just prior to this point in the session.

Therapist: Okay, give me a rating. What are your SUDs now?

Client: About three, maybe even two and a half.

Therapist: Good, again it appears that you are getting good control of the relaxation response, which will serve you well in the exposure work we are about to begin. Okay, let's begin some imaginal exposure work. As we discussed earlier, I want you to begin imagining the events that took place about nine months ago when you were shot. Once you have begun to visualize the events, I'd like you to turn on the soundtrack to a Freddie Kruger horror movie that is associated with the images, and purposely push yourself to between five to six SUDs. Let me know when you get there, and then I'll help you apply the anxiety-management techniques to calm yourself back down to about four- or four-and-a-half SUDs or so. Then we will repeat this stress-relax sequence three or four more times. Again, as we discussed earlier, it is very important to apply the CAP principle in conducting this exposure exercise. That is, you want to challenge yourself by confronting the feared memory and push yourself to between five to six SUDs, but no more than that. Then, once challenged, you should apply the anxiety-management techniques you have learned to calm yourself back down. And then, perhaps most importantly, practice calming yourself down repeatedly. With repetition, you should notice both a desensitization effect and a coping effect.

Okay, switch on the visual images having to do with the shooting, the hottest part of your memory. Let's begin with you headed from work in your car at night toward the ATM machine. Switch that portion of the memory on. Can you visualize it clearly? Describe it out loud.

Client: Yes, I can see it very clearly, almost as if it was yesterday. I'm getting out of my car. It's dark. I'm thinking about my brother coming for a visit. I walk maybe fifteen yards to the ATM. I can see the ATM there on the wall of the bank; I get 160 dollars out; I count it, put it in my pocket, and head back to my car. I see the guy out of the corner of my eye. He's walking very quickly toward me. I turn my head. He's a big guy, dressed in black. He's got a gun pointed at me. He doesn't say anything, he just shoots me. I can see the flash. My SUDs are up there now. I'm thinking I'm going to have another panic attack.

Therapist: Your SUDs?

Client: About six.

Therapist: Okay, now begin calming yourself down. Begin by distancing yourself from the visual images and blocking the thoughts about a panic attack by using the eye-movement technique. With your eyes closed now, direct yourself through a set of twenty to twenty-five eye movements.

The client completed a set of self-directed eye movements at this point.

Therapist: Your SUDs?

Client: They've come down some, about five now.

Therapist: Good, the eye-movement technique seems to have helped some. Now, follow the eye-movement technique up with an abbreviated relaxation response. Again, begin by focusing on your breathing, slowing it down, taking a normal breath, holding it briefly, and then exhaling slowly and saying "relax" silently to yourself two or three times between breaths. Air in, and now out slowly, relax, relax. And now scan your muscle groups, check to make sure no tension has developed. If it has, just take a moment or two and let it go. Check your right foot and leg. Now check your left foot and leg, stomach muscles, right arm and hand, left arm and hand, neck and shoulder muscles, forehead as smooth as a pane of glass, eyes, jaw, mouth, very, very relaxed. And once again check your breathing, taking the air in, holding it briefly, and now out slowly, saying "relax" to yourself two or three times between breaths. Air in, now out, relax, relax, relax. Your SUDs?

Client: They've come down some, about four and a half now.

Therapist: Good, the relaxation response should also prove to be a useful anxiety-management technique for you. Now add some rational thinking that we talked about before, such as, "This is just a memory. I was in danger then, but I survived and I'm safe now. I'm beginning to get control of my anxiety, and will get even greater control with practice. I didn't do anything wrong, I behaved in a reasonable fashion. Sometimes bad things do happen to good people."

Therapist: Your SUDs?

Client: They're down around four now.

Therapist: Good. You've demonstrated to both of us that you can effectively control your distress using this combination of anxiety-management techniques. Now I'd like you to get some repetitions in. Remember the third rule of the CAP principle—practice, practice, practice. There simply is no substitute for repetitive exposure trials. Okay then, challenge yourself once again by switching on the hot images having to do with the shooting and purposely push yourself back up to five to six SUDs with the images and the irrational self-talk. Go ahead. Let me know when you're back up into the five to six SUDs range.

Client: Okay, I'm there, five and a half SUDs and climbing.

Therapist: Okay, now begin calming yourself down using this combination of techniques. That is, begin with the eye-movement technique, follow that up with an abbreviated relaxation response, and then add some rational reassuring thoughts. Remember there is no right or wrong way to do this. Simply use whatever works best for you. Go ahead, let me know when you've got yourself back down to the four- to four-and-a-half SUDs range or as low as you think you are going to go.

The client coped with the distress by way of the eye-movement technique, the relaxation response, and rational thinking at this point.

Client: Okay, I'm back down to four and a half SUDs.

Therapist: Good, again notice how you are getting control of your distress. How did you do it this time? Did you use all three of the anxiety-management techniques?

Client: Yes, the combination seems to work for me. The eye-movement technique seems to help a lot, and the relaxation response also is quite helpful. The rational thinking doesn't seem to add a whole lot. Oh, maybe it helps some, but certainly not as much as the eye-movement technique and the relaxation response.

Therapist: Yes, that's what most people find at first. However, most people find that the rational thinking turns out to be the most powerful of the anxiety-management techniques over time. The eye-movement technique and the relaxation response serve as sort of bridges to help get them to the point that their rational self-talk is sufficient to manage their distress. So even though the rational thinking isn't of much help right now, I'd like you to keep using it as part of your anxiety-management strategy. Okay? Make sense?

Client: Yes.

Therapist: Good, I'd like you to get four or five exposure trials in this session and on the tape, which you should be able to use as a guide in your next homework assignment. So, once again, switch on the hot images of yourself there in the dark walking away from the ATM machine and seeing a large man dressed in black pointing a gun at you. Got it? Now add some irrational self-talk such as "Oh, no," which means, "Oh, no. I'm going to die or I'm going to have a panic attack" and purposely push yourself to between five and six SUDs. Let me know when you're there.

Client: Okay, I'm there, five and a half.

Therapist: Good. Start the calming process, beginning with the eye-movement technique. Follow the eye-movement technique up with an abbreviated relaxation response, and be sure to add in some rational thoughts such as "I'm safe, this is just a memory. I'm getting greater and greater control of my anxiety. There's no certainty that I will have a panic attack." Go ahead. Let me know when you're back down to the four- to four-and-a-half SUDs range or as low as you think you are going to go.

The client coped with the distress by applying the eye-movement technique, the relaxation response, and rational thinking at this point.

Client: Okay, I'm back down to four and a half SUDs.

Therapist: Good. Again, it looks like you're beginning to get some control of your anxiety.

In the session, the therapist went on to direct the client through a total of five brief-exposure trials, with the therapist relinquishing more and more responsibility to the client for structuring each subsequent exposure trial. The brief-exposure exercise was also recorded, and the recording was used by the client to guide herself through her next homework assignment.

Session Summary

At the conclusion of each session, summarize the main points of critical issues that surfaced in the course of the session.

Feedback

After summarizing a session—and especially after negotiating a homework assignment with the client—it is always important to ask if he or she has any questions. This not only reinforces the educational endeavors that were conducted in the session, but also underscores the collaborative nature of the therapeutic relationship.

Homework

Homework for the sessions in this phase involves inducing the relaxation response as a form of meditation, applying all three emotion-focused coping devices to control affective arousal generated by encounters with trauma-related stimuli, and conducting brief-exposure exercises to rehearse coping with trauma-related stimuli. A typical weekly assignment involves practicing the relaxation response five times as a form of meditation and conducting five imaginal brief-exposure exercises. The assignments should be written down as well as given verbally to the client. The assignments for this phase are listed below in their preferred order of occurrence.

1. Continue to practice inducing the relaxation response as a form of meditation daily.

2. Continue to use the combination of the eye-movement technique, the relaxation response, and rational thinking as emotion-focused coping devices this week whenever your distress gets into the five to six SUDs range, particularly when these emotional reactions are triggered by encounters with trauma-related stimuli.

3. Conduct at least three, and preferably five or more, imaginal brief-exposure exercises using the tape we made in here today to structure the exercises. You can also do it on your own without the aid of the tape, if you prefer. That should give you about twenty-five exposure trials this week. Be sure to apply the CAP principle throughout these exercises. Expect to see a coping effect and possibly a desensitization effect develop toward the end of the week.

4. Conduct at least three, and preferably five or more, in vivo brief-exposure exercises this week with at least five exposure trials per exercise. That is, I want you to approach a situation related to your traumatic experience in real life [specify]. I want you to expose yourself to these trauma-related environmental stimuli, conjure up the visual memory and irrational thoughts embedded in your traumatic memory, and purposely push yourself to between five and six SUDs. No more than that, now. Then, once challenged, I want you to apply the three emotion-focused coping devices you have mastered to reduce the distress to about four SUDs or so. Then I want you to repeat this calm/stress/calm sequence at least five to ten times—more if you have the time. Be sure to apply the CAP principle throughout. Expect to see coping and desensitization effects toward the end of the week.

Prolonged Exposure and Assimilation Work

Sessions 12 and 13

Objective:

The objective of this phase is to further reduce the clients' emotional reactivity to trauma-related stimuli by way of prolonged-exposure exercises. Brief-exposure exercises should have already produced strong coping and moderate desensitization effects. This exposure work focuses not only on the clients' traumatic memories but on related environmental and somatic stimuli as well. Strong desensitization effects are normally produced by this process, which should reduce the chances of a relapse.

Range of Sessions:

2–3 sessions are normally required.

Goals:

- Review current status
- Review homework
- Set agenda for the session

- Psychoeducation: basic principles of titrated prolonged-exposure work
- Skill-building: transitioning between exposure strategies
- Session summary
- Feedback
- Homework—Imaginal/in vivo prolonged exposure

Monitoring of Current Status

Again, review the clients' overall psychosocial functioning near the outset of each of the sessions in this phase. Occasionally, some supportive problem-solving may be required to address problems that have arisen before treatment of the clients' PTSD can be resumed. Questions should be asked about the prevalence and vexatiousness of the client's PTSD and related symptoms in the previous week. This can also be accomplished by administering a self-assessment instrument such as the Brief Symptom Inventory (Derogatis and Melisaratos 1983), the questionnaire in the introduction, or the Modified PTSD Symptom Scale found in appendix B. This creates the expectation that some therapeutic gains will soon begin to be realized, and it also monitors treatment progress.

Review Homework

Again, review the results of the clients' previous homework assignments near the outset of each of the sessions in this phase. Normally, these homework assignments involve inducing the relaxation response as a form of meditation, utilizing the three emotion-focused coping skills to cope with distress arising from encounters with trauma-related stimuli, and conducting prolonged-exposure exercises targeting trauma-related stimuli. The amount and proficiency of the clients' exposure homework should be carefully reviewed. Strong desensitization effects should be expected and suggested. The reasons for any noncompliance with a homework assignment should be examined and corrected, if possible. In this process, several important clinical concepts are usually reviewed, including the SUD scale, the CAP principle, and coping/desensitization effects.

Agenda

Again, the sessions in this phase should begin by asking the client to restate the overarching treatment goals: "What is it you are trying to accomplish here and how long should it take?" Again, set the agenda for each of the sessions based on the reviews of the clients' current status and homework assignments. Normally, another prolonged-exposure exercise is conducted and/or an in vivo exposure exercise is planned.

Concepts and Skills

Psycheducation

Basic Principles of Titrated Prolonged-Exposure Work

The majority of each session in this phase is taken up with an imaginal prolonged-exposure exercise and/or the planning of an in vivo exposure exercise. The principles of titrated prolonged exposure are also reviewed. Imaginal prolonged-exposure exercises conducted in the session are normally recorded, and the recording is used to structure the clients' subsequent homework assignments. The basic principles of titrated prolonged-exposure strategies are as follows.

1. Conduct prolonged-exposure work with clients once strong coping effects, and at least moderate desensitization effects, have accrued by way of brief-exposure work. This will decrease the chances that a prolonged-exposure trial will provoke an overwhelming level of distress in clients, which is generally considered to be six and a half SUDs or more.

2. During the clients' prolonged-exposure trials, emphasize the catastrophic or irrational appraisals embedded in the clients' feared stimulus complex, which quite often must be inferred from the clients' automatic thoughts and excessive distress.

3. Conduct imaginal prolonged-exposure trials to the clients' entire feared stimulus complex before conducting in vivo prolonged-exposure trials to their entire feared stimulus complex to insure that the in vivo prolonged-exposure trials are unlikely to provoke overwhelming levels of distress in the clients.

4. Once a prolonged-exposure trial is initiated, it should continue until the clients report that their distress has substantially decreased from what it was at the beginning of their prolonged-exposure trial. Ideally, this decrease in distress should be at least 50 percent of what it was at the outset. For instance, clients reporting six SUDs at the outset of a prolonged-exposure trial should continue until they report their SUDs have dropped to about four and a half or below. Three SUDs is considered "normal," or "no distress" on this scale. Typically, the duration of a titrated prolonged-exposure trial is about thirty minutes initially, with the duration usually dropping to fifteen minutes or less over the course of the next two or three prolonged-exposure trials.

5. Encourage the clients to use rational thinking during their prolonged exposure trials to manage their distress, but discourage them from using the eye-movement technique and the relaxation response to manage distress until they experience the desired 50 percent decrease in their SUDs. This insures that the distraction and suppression processes inherent in the relaxation response and the eye-movement technique do not dilute the prolonged-exposure trials and thereby inhibit the desired desensitization

ffects from developing (Wegner and Erber 1992; Wegner et al. 1987; Wenzlaff, Wegner, and Roper 1988).

A prolonged-exposure trial should be terminated, utilizing any and all of a client's cognitive coping skills, should it appear that the trial is going to overwhelm the client with excessively high levels of distress. Additional brief-exposure trials may be required in such instances before undertaking another prolonged-exposure trial, and/or a smaller subset of the client's feared stimulus complex may need to be selected for subsequent prolonged exposure trials.

Skill-Building

Transitioning Between Exposure Strategies

Following are the three basic principles of moving between strategies.

1. Always conduct brief-exposure work with clients before conducting prolonged exposure work with them.

2. Always preface in vivo exposure work with imaginal exposure work. Occasionally, this principle must be overlooked when clients cannot utilize imaginal processes to produce the distress necessary for the exposure work.

3. Move from imaginal brief-exposure work to in vivo brief-exposure work and/or imaginal prolonged-exposure work, and then move on to in vivo prolonged-exposure work. Occasionally this principle may be overlooked when clients prefer to move rapidly into in vivo exposure work due to time or monetary constraints.

Following is an excerpt from Smyth (1998e; 1998f; see appendix C) illustrating how imaginal prolonged-exposure work was conducted in the treatment of the woman who had been shot at the ATM (see Phase IV).

Therapist: Okay, you've done quite a bit of imaginal brief-exposure work with the memory of the shooting and with the unusual sensations that used to provoke your panic attacks. And this exposure work has paid off with the development of both substantial coping and substantial desensitization effects to the visual memory and to the sensations. What I'd recommend at this point is what is called a prolonged-exposure exercise, where you review your memory for a prolonged period of time, rather than for brief periods of time as you have been doing. Prolonged exposure should further reduce the distress you are experiencing when recollecting the memory by further strengthening the desensitization effects that have already developed. In this way, you should reduce the risk of relapse—where the panic attacks return or the memory again acquires the ability to elicit excessive amounts of distress. Prolonged exposure is kind of an insurance policy that seems to greatly reduce the risk of a relapse; I almost always recommend it to my clients as they near completion of their brief-exposure work. What do you think, willing to give it a try?

Client: Well, yes, I think so, but how does it differ from what I have been doing?

Therapist: Well, the main difference is that I want you to imagine the shooting again, and add the soundtrack to the Freddie Kruger horror story that is triggered by these images, the automatic thoughts such as "Oh, no" and "I've got to get out of here," and then recollect it as vividly as possible for about thirty minutes or so, rather than for a brief period of time as you have been doing. While recollecting the memory, your SUDs may go up into the five to six SUDs range, which is where I want you to try to keep it. Sooner or later, however, you're going to find that you can't maintain this moderate level of distress and your SUDs will begin to drop. Once your SUDs have dropped to around four to four and a half, then I'd like you to polish them off using the eye-movement technique and abbreviated relaxation response, but not before. You can and should use rational thinking throughout, however. This prolonged-exposure process should really enhance the desensitization effects you have been developing; you should find that no matter how hard you try, you will not be able to kick your SUDs beyond four and a half or so after a few prolonged-exposure exercises. Willing to give it a try?

Client: Yes. I guess the only difference is that I'm not going to be repeatedly calming myself down once I get to six SUDs. Is that right?

Therapist: Yes, that's correct. I think you're going to have a bit of difficulty generating six SUDs, however, given all the brief-exposure work you have done. But that is exactly what I want you to do. Try to kick up six SUDs and sustain it as long as you can. Then once your SUDs begin to drop on their own accord, say after twenty minutes or so, go ahead and reduce them even further by way of the eye-movement technique and relaxation response, but not before you experience that naturally occurring drop in your SUDs. Okay?

Client: Okay.

Therapist: Go ahead, close your eyes. I'd like to record this prolonged-exposure exercise on tape so that you can use it as a guide to conduct some more prolonged-exposure exercises on your own between now and next time we meet. Okay? What are your SUDs?

Client: About four.

Therapist: Good. Now I'd like you to begin recollecting the events leading up to the shooting. Imagine yourself in your car, driving home after working late. It's dark out, about nine o'clock; you're in your car. Describe to me out loud what your car looks like, what you're thinking about.

Client: I'm in my Honda. It's a stick shift. The seats are gray, and I've got some paperwork from the office sitting in the passenger seat. There are a couple CDs there also, and some trash on the floor, a coffee cup. The dash is gray and lit up. My lights are on. I'm thinking about my brother who's coming for a visit. I'm looking forward to seeing him again. It's been over a year since I saw him last.

Therapist: What's the traffic like? What's the scenery like?

Client: It's fairly light traffic, only a few cars on the road. There are still a couple of cars in the parking lot, but all of the stores are closed, except for the liquor store. The bank is closed. There's no one outside. The ATM on the side of the bank is all lit up.

Therapist: Give me a SUDs rating.

Client: Oh, maybe four and a half at the most. It just doesn't bother me like it use to.

Therapist: Okay, good. Now, visualize yourself pulling into the parking lot next to the ATM. Describe the ATM and how you got out of your car and went to the ATM to withdraw some money.

Client: I pull into the parking lot, park my car maybe fifteen yards from the ATM. I can see myself walking toward the ATM. It's all lit up. I can see the buttons and the screen. I put my card in, punch in my code, and get 160 dollars out. I count it, put it in my front pocket, and I head back toward my car.

Therapist: SUDs?

Client: Four and a half.

Therapist: Okay, good. What happens next?

Client: I see this guy out of the corner of my eye. He's walking very quickly toward me. I turn my head. He's a big guy, he's got a black or maybe brown sweatshirt on and lighter colored pants, tan, I think. He's got a gun pointed right at me. He doesn't say anything. He just shoots me.

Therapist: SUDs?

Client: Five or so.

Therapist: Okay, now add the automatic thoughts we know to be associated with this memory, the "Oh, no. I've got to get out of here. I'm going to panic," and try to push yourself to six SUDs. SUDs?

Client: Still about five, maybe five and a half. They just don't go up like they use to.

Therapist: Good, all that brief-exposure work is paying off. Now autosuggest the somatic sensations, the chest pressure and the feeling that you can't get your breath. Got them? SUDs?

Client: It's hard to produce those sensations anymore, but I can still get them, just not as strong as before. Five and a half, almost six SUDs now.

Therapist: Okay, good. Notice how much more difficult it is to produce the sensations as well as the SUDs now. Seems that the brief-exposure work has really done its job. Okay, I want you to try to sustain the six SUDs for as long as you can. My guess is that your SUDs will begin dropping on their own accord in fifteen to twenty minutes or so, maybe a half an hour at the most. Let me add in all the irrational meanings that probably lie behind the automatic thoughts and phrases as you continue to imagine the gun, the shooter, the ATM. "I'm going to die. I'm certain to panic. I have no control. I'm going to be humiliated. People will think I'm crazy."

You can counter these irrational thoughts with more realistic or rational ones as I state them, but hold off on using the eye-movement technique and the relaxation response until you notice that drop off in your SUDs, which should occur in a while. Okay, visualize the gun, the shooter. Look at his brown or black sweatshirt, his tan pants, look at the gun in his right hand, it's a small, silver gun. Add in the sound track to the Freddie Kruger horror story. "Oh, no. I'm certain to die. I'm certain to have a panic attack. What's wrong with me, people will think I'm crazy." Now what's wrong with each of these statements? What's wrong with, "I'm certain to die"?

Client: This is just a memory. I was in danger then, but I survived. I'm safe now.

Therapist: What's wrong with, "I'm certain to have a panic attack"?

Client: There's no certainty I'll have one. I've learned what causes those unusual sensations, and I've proved to myself many times now that I can have these sensations and they won't cause me to have a panic attack. They're not dangerous sensations, just unusual sensations.

Therapist: And what's wrong with, "I'll be humiliated. People will think I'm crazy"?

Client: Well, it's not likely that I'll have a panic attack, and even if I did, people wouldn't think ill of me. Even if they did, so what, they'll get over it.

Therapist: And what about, "I don't have any control over my distress. I've got to run away"?

Client: I do have some control. I've proved that many, many times in the brief-exposure exercises; and I'll get even more control with continued exposure work.

Therapist: And what about, "I must have done something terribly wrong to have deserved this"?

Client: Well, it's not true. I didn't do anything wrong. I acted in a reasonable fashion. I was just at the wrong place at the wrong time. Sometimes bad things do happen to good people.

Therapist: Good. Focus on the visual images now. See the shooter, the gun, the ATM. Now the unusual sensations—the chest pressure and feeling that you can't catch your breath. Add in the automatic thoughts, the "Oh, no. I've got to get out of here. I can't stand this. I'm going to die." Now add the meaning behind these thoughts, the "I've got absolutely no control over my distress. I'm certain to have one of those god-awful panic attacks. People are certain to think I'm crazy, and that would be just awful, something which I could never recover from. The only way I can possibly handle this is to run away. I must have done something terribly wrong." Your SUDs?

Client: Still up around five and a half.

Therapist: Good, stick with it. I'd expect that drop in your SUDs to occur sometime in the next fifteen or twenty minutes, just stay with it. Try to keep your SUDs as close to six for as long as you can. Describe to me the shooter again, and the ATM, and your automatic thoughts, and your autosuggested sensations.

Client: It's dark out. I'm in front of the ATM. It's all lit up, but everything else around it is dark. I can see its buttons and its screen. I've got some slacks and a blouse on. My jacket is in the car. My car is fifteen to twenty yards away, the parking lot is all but empty. All the stores are closed except for the liquor store at the far end of the mall. I put my card in, punch my code in, and get 160 dollars out. I see myself counting it in front of the ATM, then I put my card and the money in my front pocket. I see the guy coming up from my left side out of the corner of my eye. I turn to walk back to my car. He's maybe ten or fifteen feet away. He doesn't say anything. He's walking fast toward me. He's got a gun in his right hand pointed right at me. He's got a brown or black sweatshirt on and tan pants. The gun is silver in color and it's not very big. He's a big guy, over six feet. He's in the shadow of the awning so I can't see his face very well. He's got a broad face and short hair. He's a white guy. I'm thinking he's going to rob me. Then he shoots me. He doesn't say anything, he just shoots. I remember spinning around and falling down after that. I guess that's how I fractured my left arm. I don't remember much after that until the police and the paramedics arrived. I remember someone bending over me, one of the paramedics, and telling me to stay calm and that I was going to make it and that they were going to take me to the hospital. I really didn't feel any pain that I can remember, but I remember thinking I was going to die and never see my brother or my parents again. I remember having difficulty breathing from all the blood. I remember waking up in the hospital, but I don't remember the trip to the hospital at all.

Therapist: SUDs?

Client: Oh, still about five and a half. It's still upsetting but not like before.

Therapist: Good, all that brief-exposure work you did has served you well. Now add in the automatic thoughts and phrases plus autosuggest the unusual sensations of chest pressure and a feeling you can't catch your breath. The "Oh, no. I've got to get out of here. I'm going crazy." Think about and create that pressure in the center of your chest. Now the sensations of having difficulty getting your breath. Tell yourself that you're certain to have a panic attack, that you have no control, that you're going to die, that you'll never see your family ever again, that you must have done something terribly wrong to deserve this. Your SUDs?

Client: Well, they've gone up some, nearly to six now.

Therapist: Good, stay with it. They will begin to drop in a while. Again notice how long it took to create this level of distress. Much longer than before. The brief-exposure work has done its job. And what's wrong with all those irrational automatic thoughts and phrases?

Client: Yes, it has. The memory doesn't bother me like it use to. It still upsets me, but I know I can calm myself down if I need to. This distress won't last forever. It's unpleasant but temporary and it won't cause me to go crazy. I'm not going to die. I was in danger then, but that was in the past, I survived and I'm safe now. I have seen my family many times since then and I will continue to see them. I'm not likely to have a panic attack. I've proven that many times before when I created those unusual sensations by way of autosuggestion. And I'm certainly not to blame; I behaved in a reasonable fashion. I was just in the wrong place at the wrong time.

Therapist: How credible do these disputes to your irrational automatic thoughts and phrases seem to you now?

Client: Very credible.

Therapist: Good, you've done a lot of work in this area and your self-talk is much more accurate and realistic now. Your SUDs?

Client: Oh, they're down some, maybe five.

Therapist: Good, stay with it and try to push them back to six, if you can. Look at the ATM again. Visualize it as clearly as you can. Look at the buttons, the screen; notice how it's all lit up. Now the shooter with his dark sweatshirt, tan pants, broad face, short hair, the gun in his hand, approaching you rapidly. Now the unusual sensations, autosuggest them, add them in. Got them?

Client: Well, as I told you before, I'm having a much harder time creating them now. I can still get them, but they're not as strong as they use to be.

Therapist: Do the best you can to create them and keep your SUDs up. SUDs?

Client: They've dropped some more, five at the very most.

Therapist: Visualize the shooting as clearly as possible and add the irrational automatic thoughts and phrases. Tell yourself that you're certain to die, that you're certain to have a panic attack, that you have absolutely no control over your distress, that you are certain to go crazy, that you will never see your family ever again, that you are to blame for this tragedy.

Client: I can still see the memory very clearly and I can say all these things to myself, but I really don't believe them anymore.

Therapist: Good, that's what is expected and hoped for. But it's still very important to repeat them to yourself while reviewing the visual memory since you can never really stop or eliminate irrational self-talk. You can certainly develop a means of neutralizing the irrational self-talk by linking it up with more realistic self-talk, which is what you are rehearsing now. SUDs?

Client: About five, or maybe a little less.

Therapist: Again, try everything to keep your SUDs as high as you can. Visualize the shooting as vividly as possible. Look at the ATM, now the shooter with his dark sweatshirt and tan pants, broad face, short hair, gun in his hand. Feel yourself spinning around from being shot, feel the sensations of having difficulty getting your breath because of all the blood. Now the unusual sensations, the chest pressure and the sensation that you can't get enough air. Now the irrational thoughts. Tell yourself that you are certain to die, that you are certain to have a panic attack, that you are certain to go crazy, that you will never see your family ever again, that you are to blame for this tragedy. SUDs?

Client: I just can't keep them up there. They're down to four and a half now.

Therapist: Good, that's what we're looking for. Notice how difficult it was to produce the SUDs in the first place, compared to when you first started your exposure work, and how, try as you might, you could only keep them in the five to six range for fifteen or twenty minutes or so. With additional prolonged exposure exercises you should find it even harder to kick your SUDs up into the five to six range and you should also find that you will not be able to keep them there very long. That is the desensitization effect that we're looking for. Once you've found your SUDs have dropped to four or four and a half or so during a prolonged-exposure exercise, go ahead and polish them off using the eye-movement technique and the relaxation response, but not before that drop in your SUDs has occurred. SUDs?

Client: Four and a half or somewhat less.

Therapist: Good. Okay, take a minute or so and calm yourself down even further using first the eye-movement technique then an abbreviated relaxation response. But before you do that, I'd like you to remind yourself that this tragedy isn't all tragedy. Some good has come of it, and what is that?

Client: Well, I now have a much greater appreciation for life. I was taking a lot of things for granted, and my priorities and values were a bit screwed up. In a strange way this helped me get me priorities back in order. Not a way I would recommend to anyone, however, but it did do that. And now I really cherish the opportunities I have had and will have, and I'll try to make the best of them, 'cause you just never know. It could all end tomorrow. I'm also a bit less trusting and optimistic, but this isn't all bad, as it will make me check out people and situations a little closer. Something I probably should have been doing all along, anyway.

Therapist: This tragedy seems to make a lot more sense to you now than it did before, and you have really integrated it into a very healthy and functional philosophy of life. A lot of hard work and pain has gone into this, so don't forget to compliment yourself for successfully completing a long and perilous journey. Okay, go ahead, now, and use the eye-movement technique and the relaxation response to calm yourself back down to three or three and a half SUDs or as low as you think you are going to go. Let me know when you're there.

The client then directed herself through a set of eye movements coupled with a self-induced abbreviated relaxation response at this point.

Client: Okay, I'm back down to three SUDs.

Therapist: Great. Both coping and desensitization effects are quite strong, but I'd still like you to do some more prolonged-exposure work to further strengthen the desensitization effect that you have been developing.

Again, in this way you will reduce the chances of a relapse in the future as well as experience the immediate benefit of a further reduction in the amount of distress the memory and associated stimuli provoke in you. You've almost accomplished what you set out to accomplish, which was to turn a hot memory into a bad memory, one that is unpleasant but no longer provokes an overwhelming amount of distress and one that you feel to be very much in control of. What do you think? Willing to do some prolonged exposure on your own?

Client: Sure, I think it should help.

Therapist: Good, how about doing four or five prolonged-exposure exercises on your own using this tape as a guide before we meet again in a week?

Client: That's fine, I shouldn't have any trouble doing that.

Therapist: Okay. In doing the prolonged exposure exercises be sure to do everything you can to keep your SUDs in the five to six range for as long as you can by using everything at your disposal—the visual memory, the sensations, the irrational automatic thoughts and phrases. Of course be sure to add in the more realistic self-talk when you are doing this, but hold off on using the eye-movement technique and the relaxation response until you notice your SUDs have dropped down to four and a half or less. Okay? Any questions? By the end of the week I doubt you will be able to provoke five to six SUDs; even if you can, I'd seriously doubt you would be able to sustain that level of distress for more than five minutes or so. And that is exactly what we're looking for—a strong desensitization effect. Okay? Let me write this down for you so you'll have something to refer to if you have any questions about it during the week.

Session Summary

At the conclusion of each session, summarize the main points of critical issues that surfaced in the course of the session.

Feedback

After summarizing a session—and especially after negotiating a homework assignment with the client—it is always important to ask if he or she has any questions. This not only reinforces the educational endeavors that were conducted in the session, but also underscores the collaborative nature of the therapeutic relationship.

Homework

Homework for the one to three sessions in this phase usually involves inducing the relaxation response as a form of meditation, applying all three emotion-focused coping devices to control excessive distress provoked by encounters with trauma-related stimuli, and conducting prolonged-exposure exercises targeting trauma-related stimuli. A typical weekly assignment might involve practicing the relaxation technique five times or more as a form of meditation and conducting five imaginal prolonged-exposure exercises. The assignments should be written down as well as given verbally to the client. The assignments for this phase are listed below in their preferred order of occurrence.

1. Continue to practice inducing the relaxation response as a form of meditation daily. Also use the relaxation response to prepare yourself for a known stressor at least twice this week.

2. Continue to use the combination of the eye-movement technique, the relaxation response, and rational thinking to cope with excessive stress reactions provoked by encounters with trauma-related stimuli.

3. Conduct at least three imaginal prolonged-exposure exercises this week using the tape we made in here today to help structure the exercises. Be sure to follow the principles of prolonged exposure. That is, try to push yourself to about six SUDs and keep yourself there for as long as possible. You can and should use rational thinking to manage your distress during the exercise, but hold off on using the eye-movement technique and the relaxation response until the desensitization effect becomes evident. That is, wait until you find you can't keep your distress at the six SUDs level anymore, and it has fallen of its own accord to about four or four and a half. Then you can go ahead and polish off your distress using the eye-movement technique and the relaxation response and terminate the exercise. But be sure to wait until the desensitization effect has occurred. Given the amount of brief-exposure work you have done, I'd expect the desensitization effect to set in after twenty or maybe thirty minutes of prolonged exposure. You should notice the desensitization effect setting in much earlier toward the end of the week—maybe after five or ten minutes of prolonged-exposure work.

4. Conduct at least three in vivo prolonged-exposure exercises this week in which you put yourself in the trauma-related situation [specify], and then review the visual memory, the thoughts, and the sensations all at the same time. Try to push yourself to six SUDs and keep yourself there for as long as possible. You can manage your distress during the exercise by way of rational thinking, but hold off on the use of the eye-movement technique and relaxation response until a desensitization effect becomes evident. That is, wait until your SUDs drop to four or four and a half or so despite all your efforts to keep them up, and then go ahead and polish off your distress using the eye-movement technique and the relaxation response and terminate the exposure trial. I'd expect the desensitization effect to set in after about thirty minutes or so, maybe sooner, given the amount of imaginal prolonged-exposure work you have done.

Relapse Prevention Work

Sessions 14 and 15

Objective:

The primary objective of this phase is to maintain the clinical gains that have been realized. This is accomplished by educating the client as to some common causes of relapse and how he or she can reduce the risk for relapse.

Range of Sessions:

1–2 sessions are usually required.

Goals:

- Review current status
- Psychoeducation: relapse prevention
- Session summary
- Feedback
- Termination

Monitoring of Current Status

In addition to treatment goals, review the prevalence and vexatiousness of the PTSD symptoms that the clients have experienced since their last session. This can also be accomplished by administering a self-assessment instrument such as the Brief Symptom Inventory (Derogatis and Melisaratos 1983), the questionnaire in the introduction, or the Modified PTSD Symptom Scale found in appendix B. Clients should be reminded that although they may have eliminated or learned to manage their PTSD symptoms well, there is always the possibility of a relapse. Point out that old irrational habits die hard and could return, and emphasize that clients should keep using their newly acquired coping skills to reduce the chances that a relapse will occur. Also, point out that if a relapse does occur it should not be taken as evidence that treatment failed. Instead, it should be heeded as an early wake-up call; a brief refresher course in cognitive-behavioral therapy may be needed.

Concepts and Skills

Psychoeducation

Relapse Prevention

One risk factor for relapse is falling back into old patterns of excessive avoidance. Other risk factors include excessive prolonged stress brought on by multiple psychosocial stressors, sleep deprivation, and substance abuse. You should emphasize the application of the CAP principle as the clients' best defense against excessive avoidance, and effective problem-solving as the clients' best defense against psychosocial stressors. Remind the clients to use emotion-focused coping techniques, coupled with the compartmentalization-of-worry technique, as good defensive strategies against excessive worry.

Session Summary

Again, at the conclusion of each session, summarize the main points of critical issues that surfaced in the course of the session.

Feedback

After summarizing a session, always ask the client if he or she has any questions. This not only reinforces the educational endeavors that were conducted in the session, but also underscores the collaborative nature of the therapeutic relationship.

Treatment Evaluation

This is a good time to ask your client to complete the Modified PTSD Symptom Scale (appendix B) so you can evaluate together the gains that have been achieved. Also ask the client to complete the Program Satisfaction Questionnaire (see next page).

Termination

Treatment should be formally terminated at the conclusion of one or two follow-up sessions, but you should emphasize that the client can return at any time for any reason, that the door is always open.

Program Satisfaction Questionnaire (PSQ)

Please evaluate the therapy program you have just completed by answering the following questions. Circle the number that best reflects your opinion. Your honest answer, whether positive or negative, will give us feedback to make the program better.

1. How effective was the therapy program in helping you with your problem?

   1   2   3   4   5   6   7
   Not effective   *Moderately effective*   *Extremely effective*

2. How helpful were the homework and exercises in this therapy program?

   1   2   3   4   5   6   7
   Not helpful   *Moderately helpful*   *Extremely helpful*

3. Were the skills you learned in this therapy program useful for coping with your problem?

   1   2   3   4   5   6   7
   Not useful   *Moderately useful*   *Extremely useful*

4. Overall, how would you rate the quality of this therapy?

   1   2   3   4   5   6   7
   High quality   *Moderate Quality*   *Low Quality*

5. If someone with a similar problem to yours asked for recommendations, how would you describe the usefulness of this therapy program?

   1   2   3   4   5   6   7
   Not useful   *Moderately useful*   *Extremely useful*

6. If you could go back to remake your decision about this therapy program, would you do it again?

   1   2   3   4   5   6   7
   No definitely   *Uncertain*   *Yes definitely*

7. How successfully were your goals met by this therapy program?

   1   2   3   4   5   6   7
   Goals met   *Moderately successful with goals*   *Goals not met*

8. How would you rate your improvement in the symptoms that concerned you most?

   1   2   3   4   5   6   7
   Extremely improved   *Moderately improved*   *Not improved*

Appendix A

Theory

Efforts have been made to explain the confusing array of symptoms that define PTSD from a biological perspective (for example, van der Kolk 1984), from a behavioral perspective (for example, Keane 1989), as well as from a psychodynamic perspective (for example, Horowitz 1986; Marmar 1991; Weiss 1993). What follows is an attempt to explain this array of symptoms in a clinically meaningful fashion from an information-processing point of view (Creamer et al. 1992; Foa and Kozak 1986) while borrowing heavily from a psychodynamic perspective as well as a cognitive-behavioral perspective in the process, particularly from Epstein (1994). Although the proffered theory utilizes computer metaphors to facilitate the explanations being offered, it is important to keep in mind that the processes being described are actually accomplished by means of biochemical processes operating within known neurological brain structures. It is also very important to keep in mind that the explanations being offered are only theoretical speculations; relatively little empirical evidence presently exists to support them (or any other theoretical explanations, for that matter).

The underlying theoretical structure of the mind guiding the cognitive-behavioral treatment of PTSD proposed herein likens the mind to a computer with three basic programs—the secondary-process program, the automatic-thinking program, and the primary-process program. All three programs operate at both the conscious and the preconscious level of awareness, and repressive-suppressive forces can be erected against any of the three programs, thereby keeping their data-processing efforts from entering conscious awareness. Memory is conceived as a database that is stored on three disks—temporary memory storage, intermediate memory storage, and long-term memory storage. Data tends to move sequentially from temporary to intermediate and then to long-term memory storage but can move from temporary to long-term storage and can move from long-term to intermediate memory storage. Data can be analyzed at any stage by any of the three programs. Data left in temporary memory will be erased after a relatively short period of time unless it's moved into the intermediate memory storage system. Once data has been transferred into intermediate memory it is unlikely to be erased unless and until the data is transferred out of this system and into long-term memory storage. This transfer cannot take place until the data has been encoded in such a way that it is perceived as currently not dangerous and as congruent with extant meta-cognitions. Meta-cognitions are large cognitive schemata comprised of assumptions and beliefs the individuals have about themselves and about the world in which they live that help them interpret complex patterns of stimuli and select coping strategies to deal with both expected and unexpected events in their lives. Data stored in the intermediate memory storage system will periodically strive for active processing by the data-processing programs since the intermediate memory storage system operates on a continuous playback loop. This insures periodic reactivations of the data, which retards erasure of the data. The long-term memory storage system, on the other hand, is a static system and data recorded in it will only be processed again if the data is intentionally retrieved by one of the three data-processing systems. Also, data stored in the long-term memory storage system will be erased if it is not periodically activated by one of the three data-processing programs. This activation can occur in the form of conscious recall of the specific data or by activation of one or more of the files in which the data has been recorded.

The secondary-process program prefers words as its primary language, operates relatively slowly, encodes data in terms of logical causal relationships, and is primarily an editing program for the automatic-thinking program, which corrects problems in the meta-cognitions and the subroutines created and run by the automatic-thinking program. The secondary-process program may also be called upon to decide which subroutine to execute when two or more subroutines are activated and judged equally viable by the automatic-thinking program. The secondary- process program accomplishes its tasks by way of abstract analytical reasoning processes. The secondary process operates optimally in conscious awareness at moderate levels of physiological arousal. It tends to operate inefficiently at either high or low levels of arousal.

The primary-process program prefers to use images to analyze data rather than words, favors encoding data in imaginal metaphors, operates relatively slowly, and operates optimally outside of awareness and at moderate levels of physiological arousal. It tends to operate during sleep in the form of dreams as a default option to unsuccessful secondary process and automatic-thinking program efforts to solve problems during the waking state. However, primary-process thinking can and does occur consciously during the waking state in some disordered states, such as schizophrenia; it can facilitate creative problem-solving endeavors during the waking state provided the primary process program is subordinate to and under the control of the secondary process (regression in the service of the ego in psychoanalytic terms). This phenomenon perhaps is best illustrated by the "aha" experience, in which a solution to a problem an individual has been consciously struggling to solve for some time by way of the secondary-process program suddenly bursts into awareness after a period of time in which the individual's conscious attention has been occupied by other matters. Clearly, such a solution could only have been reached by way of a high-level abstract-reasoning process, but try as that individual might, the processes used to reach the solution cannot be brought into conscious awareness. Conversely, the secondary-process and automatic-thinking programs sometimes operate during dreams to the exclusion of the primary process, such as in the nightmares of trauma victims in which their traumatic experiences are vividly and veridically recalled. The primary-process program, like the secondary-process program, employs abstract-reasoning processes to problem-solve data, but the imaginal language used in the reasoning process is in the form of highly idiosyncratic metaphors. The plasticity of the imaginal metaphors is the strength of the primary process program, for this can sometimes overcome functional sets blocking problem-solving that have been created by the secondary process' reliance on words.

The automatic-thinking program employs both words and concrete images to process data, favors encoding data by association (proximity in time, space, and physical attributes) as opposed to making rational causal connections, operates relatively quickly, usually operates at the preconscious level of awareness, and tends to encode data dicotomously (good/bad, right/wrong, villain/victim). Its forte is complex-pattern recognition, for example, it enables the individual to quickly recognize and categorize gestalts made up of multiple internal and external stimuli. Compared to those established by the secondary- and primary-process programs, codes established by the automatic-thinking program are more impervious to change and tend to become cemented with repetition. The automatic-thinking program operates efficiently at low, moderate, and high levels of physiological arousal and tends to displace the secondary-process program from conscious awareness at high levels of arousal. The automatic-thinking program is responsible for creating and modifying meta-cognitions, which are long chains of bits of data that have been analyzed by all three data-processing programs and linked together by means of the automatic-thinking program's rules of association. This program is also responsible for executing well-rehearsed subroutines embedded in the meta-cognitions, for example, directing the large number of complex sequential behaviors necessary to drive a car safely after having overlearned the behavior, or directing well-rehearsed complex chains of social behavior. The automatic-thinking program also has the responsibility of encoding data stored in temporary memory as to its subject matter (survival, procreation, self); whether it is "important/unimportant," "dangerous/safe," or "congruent/incongruent" (with existing meta-cognitions); and whether it should "process again now" or "process again later." When data is encoded in conscious awareness as "process again later," the data is considered suppressed, whereas it is considered repressed when the data is encoded as such outside of conscious awareness. The automatic-thinking program is also responsible for downloading the intermediate-memory storage system, which it often does during sleep, by first organizing all data held in the system that has been encoded as important, safe, and congruent into appropriate categories and then transferring the batched data into the files of the appropriate meta-cognitions. Data that is incongruent or not safe must be processed further by one or more of the data-processing programs during the day or at night during dreams. In primary-process-dominated dreams, the individual is thought to be trying to use the plasticity of the primary process' imaginal metaphors to reframe "stuck" data into a variety of categories to find a good fit with extant meta-cognitions and/or to be trying out a variety of novel solutions when the solutions found in the meta-cognitions don't seem to be working very well. In automatic-thinking-program-dominated dreams such as those of trauma victims who veridically recall their traumatic experiences, the individual is thought to be attempting to make sense of incongruent data and/or searching for novel solutions but doing so by way of the secondary-process program, and in addition the individual is thought to be attempting to access a natural desensitization process built into the species that helps humans master traumatic experiences. More specifically, humans are thought to be biologically predisposed to repeatedly expose themselves to traumatic stimuli in a relaxed state brought on by sleep. This natural desensitization paradigm is thought capable of "extinguishing" the fear associated with traumatic stimuli, provided sufficient repetition occurs. Many cases of acute PTSD that spontaneously remit are believed to do so, in part, because of this natural desensitization process. In the case of chronic PTSD, this process is thought to go awry because alcohol, drugs, or medication hamper the process and/or because the traumatic stimuli recapitulated in the dreams provoke excessively intense distress that awakens the individual, thereby prematurely terminating the reexposure trial and precluding any desensitization effects from accruing.

Meta-cognitions are stored in the long-term memory storage system and organize data analyzed by all three data-processing systems. The meta-cognitions are created by the automatic-thinking program and the data contained in each of the meta-cognitions is organized by way of the automatic-thinking program's associational logic. The cognitions are organized around several universal high-order needs or motives, including the desire to physically survive, the desire for the psychological self to survive, the desire to experience pleasure, the desire to procreate, and the desire to be bonded with and valued by others. Abridged versions of these meta-cognitions—called cognitive templates—are located in temporary memory storage, which the automatic-thinking program uses to encode the new data entering the system with regard to category, importance, dangerousness, and congruency. The cognitive templates highlight the most salient elements of the meta-cognitions and enable individuals to quickly make sense of the massive amount of information that is constantly entering their database. The cognitive templates also enable individuals to quickly plot a preferred course of action to be taken with regard to the incoming data from among the multiple subroutines found within the meta-cognitions.

The intrusive thoughts, nightmares, and flashbacks characteristic of clients with PTSD can be explained as data "stuck" in the intermediate memory storage system that has been encoded as "important" and "dangerous." The data may also be encoded as incongruent with existing meta-cognitions, depending on the nature of the trauma as well as on the clients' preexisting meta-cognitions. The data will remain "stuck" until it is processed by the secondary-process program and/or the primary-process program, and the codes are changed to "safe, not currently dangerous" and "congruent" with existing meta-cognitions. Incongruent data is made congruent by the secondary-process program (or possibly the primary-process program) changing or refining the automatic-thinking program's initial appraisals of the data and/or by the secondary-process program (or possibly the primary-process program) making changes in the meta-cognitions that enable the previously discordant data to be assimilated. The data will also continue to periodically demand processing, intrude into conscious awareness, and provoke intense emotional distress as long as it remains "stuck" in intermediate memory. In most cases of PTSD, the traumatic memories are initially coded as "dangerous" because of an actual threat to the individual's life, but later they are coded "dangerous" because of their ability to elicit high levels of psychological distress. These theoretical speculations have much in common with those of Horowitz (1986), who explained the repetitive nature of the reexperiencing symptoms of PTSD on the basis of traumatic memories being stuck in "active memory" because of their incongruence with the individual's overarching cognitive "schemata."

The therapeutic task in eliminating PTSD reexperiencing symptoms is believed to be the facilitation of the transfer of data stuck in the intermediate-memory storage system to the meta-cognitions stored in the long-term-memory storage system. In order to accomplish this, the codes imposed on the data by the automatic-thinking program must be changed from "dangerous and incongruent" to "safe, not currently dangerous" and "congruent," which is best accomplished by accessing the secondary-process program while the traumatic data is in conscious awareness. The problem, of course, is that high levels of physiological arousal frequently are precipitated by the activation of the traumatic memories, which in turn enervates the automatic-thinking program and neutralizes the secondary-process program. However, if cognitive-behavioral exposure strategies can successfully enable the client to recode the data to "safe, not currently dangerous" and thereby keep physiological arousal in the moderate range, efforts can be made to revise how the traumatic memories are encoded to make them more congruent with existing meta-cognitions and/or the meta-cognitions themselves can be modified to accept the encoded traumatic memories. Once encoded as "safe" and "congruent," the memories will be transferred out of the intermediate-memory storage system and the repetitive reexperiencing symptoms should cease.

The hyperarousal symptoms of PTSD (irritability, sleep disturbance, exaggerated startle response, hypervigilance) are viewed as a direct consequence of the individual receiving severe emotional "shocks" whenever the traumatic memories are activated because these shocks are frequent, unpredictable, and uncontrollable, which makes life appear to be constantly dangerous, even in sleep. The avoidant symptoms of PTSD are thought of as coping efforts designed to reduce the chances that environmental stimuli associated with the traumatic memories will be encountered that could trigger unwanted recollections of the traumatic memories and/or reduce the chances that the individual will unexpectedly lose emotional control and be humiliated or harm someone in certain social settings. These fears tend to generalize and become associated with an even greater range of stimuli, particularly endogenous cues, and over time the individual tends to become anxious about being anxious. Generalized anxiety disorder and/or panic disorder can be the result. Efforts to cope with and adapt to the reexperiencing symptoms plus the additional anxiety disorders that do develop take a variety of forms, with substance abuse being one of the most common. Numbing symptoms are thought to be a form of depression that is largely explained on the basis of frequent conscious appraisals reflecting a sense of helplessness, hopelessness, worthlessness, and/or grave loss with regard to the self, the world, the future, and with regard to the PTSD symptoms. The client's PTSD-inspired avoidant behavior is also thought to contribute to the numbing/depressive symptoms by reducing the frequency with which the client engages in pleasant activities, particularly pleasant social activities. A host of vocational and interpersonal problems can also develop, with the extent and type of these problems depending in part on the premorbid functioning of the client and on his posttrauma environment. In the most severe cases of maladaptation, trauma-induced personality disorders principally of the paranoid, avoidant, borderline, and antisocial types can develop over time in predisposed individuals.

In summary, PTSD is conceptualized as an interlocking set of specific and social phobias, the primary one being a fear of memories. Over time, these phobias frequently contribute to the development of additional anxiety disorders, including panic disorder and generalized anxiety disorder. Efforts to cope with the phobias and any additional anxiety disorders that develop commonly take the form of avoidance/escape behaviors characteristic of PTSD. PTSD-induced social phobias tend to be of the generalized type, with underlying fears of losing control of intense rage and/or fears of having panic attacks that will prove to be humiliating. The hyperarousal symptoms of PTSD are accounted for by the unpredictable, frequent, and severe nature of the emotional "shocks" the individual receives whenever their traumatic memories are activated; danger is always afoot. The memories themselves, which typically remind the individual of how dangerous life can be, also contribute to this hypervigilant hyperaroused state. The PTSD avoidant behavior persists because the behavior does reduce the frequency of the "shocks" an individual receives by reducing the individual's exposure to environmental cues that serve as retrieval cues for the traumatic memories. Many shocks are unpredictable and unavoidable, however, because the traumatic memories are stored in the intermediate-memory storage system, which periodically replays all data stored in it. Repressive-suppressive forces can be erected against memories stored in this system that will reduce the frequency of the shocks somewhat, but such solutions are usually temporary and highly variable in effectiveness, giving rise to the waxing and waning of reexperiencing symptoms commonly observed in PTSD. The traumatic memories will remain stuck in the intermediate-memory storage system, thereby subjecting the individual to repetitive reexperiencing symptoms until such time as the memories have been encoded as "safe" and as "congruent" with the individual's extant meta-cognitions. This encoding change is best accomplished by way of the secondary-process program. The primary therapeutic task in PTSD treatment then becomes the activation of the traumatic memories while keeping physiological arousal in the moderate range so that the secondary-process program can effectively rewrite the original codes created by the automatic-thinking program to classify the traumatic memories, and/or the secondary-process program can be used to revise the meta-cognitions that the traumatic material contradict. The techniques thought to best accomplish this therapeutic task are the same techniques that have been found to be effective against generalized anxiety disorder, panic disorder, and phobias in general: prolonged-exposure strategies coupled with brief-exposure strategies that emphasize the importance of correcting irrational self-talk such as anxiety-management training (Suinn 1990) and stress-inoculation training (Meichenbaum 1985). Important to keep in mind, however, is the fact that these cognitive-behavioral exposure strategies are thought to work because of their impact on cognitions as well as on classically conditioned anxiety. Once the codes have been corrected, the recoded data must still be appropriately filed within one or more meta-cognition, and this filing process is facilitated by conscious secondary-process-dominated storytelling (Meichenbaum 1985).

Modified PTSD Symptom Scale

Developed by Sherry Falsetti, Heidi Resnick, Patricia Resick & Dean Kilpatrick
Medical University of South Carolina & University of Missouri—St. Louis

Instructions: The purpose of this scale is to measure the frequency and severity of symptoms in <u>the past two weeks</u>. Using the scale below, please indicate the frequency of symptoms to the left of each item. Then indicate the severity beside each item by circling the letter that fits you best.

FREQUENCY

0 = Not at all

1 = Once per week or less/a little bit/once in a while

2 = 2 to 4 times per week/somewhat/half the time

3 = 5 or more times per week/very much/almost always

SEVERITY

A = Not at all distressing

B = A little bit distressing

C = Moderately distressing

D = Quite a bit distressing

E = Extremely distressing

FREQUENCY

_____ 1. Have you had recurrent or intrusive distressing thoughts or recollections about the event(s)?

_____ 2. Have you been having recurrent bad dreams or nightmares about the event(s)?

_____ 3. Have you had the experience of suddenly reliving the event(s), flashbacks of it, acting or feeling as if it were re-occurring?

SEVERITY

A B C D E

A B C D E

A B C D E

FREQUENCY

0 = Not at all

1 = Once per week or less/a little bit/once in a while

2 = 2 to 4 times per week/somewhat/half the time

3 = 5 or more times per week/very much/almost always

SEVERITY

A = Not at all distressing

B = A little bit distressing

C = Moderately distressing

D = Quite a bit distressing

E = Extremely distressing

FREQUENCY   **SEVERITY**

_____ 4. Have you been intensely emotionally upset when reminded of the event(s) (includes anniversary reactions)?   A   B   C   D   E

_____ 5. Have you persistently been making efforts to avoid thoughts or feelings associated with the event(s) we've talked about?   A   B   C   D   E

_____ 6. Have you persistently been making efforts to avoid activities, situations, or places that remind you of the event(s)?   A   B   C   D   E

_____ 7. Are there any important aspects about the event(s) that you still cannot recall?   A   B   C   D   E

_____ 8. Have you markedly lost interest in free time activities since the event(s)?   A   B   C   D   E

_____ 9. Have you felt detached or cut off from others around you since the event(s)?   A   B   C   D   E

_____ 10. Have you felt that your ability to experience emotions is less (e.g., unable to have loving feelings, feeling numb, can't cry when sad, etc.)?   A   B   C   D   E

_____ 11. Have you felt that any future plans or hopes have changed because of the event(s) (e.g., no career, marriage, children, or long life)?   A   B   C   D   E

_____ 12. Have you been having persistent difficulty falling or staying asleep?   A   B   C   D   E

_____ 13. Have you been continuously irritable or having anger outbursts?   A   B   C   D   E

FREQUENCY	SEVERITY
0 = Not at all	A = Not at all distressing
1 = Once per week or less/a little bit/once in a while	B = A little bit distressing
2 = 2 to 4 times per week/somewhat/half the time	C = Moderately distressing
3 = 5 or more times per week/very much/almost always	D = Quite a bit distressing
	E = Extremely distressing

FREQUENCY   **SEVERITY**

_____ 14. Have you been having persistent difficulty concentrating?   A B C D E

_____ 15. Are you overly alert (e.g., check to see who is around you) since the event(s)?   A B C D E

_____ 16. Have you been jumpier, more easily startled, since the event(s)?   A B C D E

_____ 17. Have you been having intense PHYSICAL REACTIONS (e.g., sweaty, heart palpitations) when reminded of the event(s)?   A B C D E

Scoring of the Modified PTSD Symptom Scale

Dichotomous Scoring

1. Determine presence versus absence of the symptoms for reexperiencing, avoidance and numbing, and arousal criteria for PTSD by counting all item frequencies scores of one or higher and corresponding severity score of at least B (a little bit distressing) as 1 = present.

2. Determine if the following criteria were met:

Criteria	MPSS items
Reexperiencing = 1 or more items endorsed	1,2,3,4,17
Avoidance/numbing = 3 or more items endorsed	5,6,7,8,9,10,11
Arousal = 2 or more items endorsed	12,13,14,15,16

Continuous Scoring

1. Score items by adding up the frequency scores, the severity scores, and then summing the frequency and severity scores for the Full Scale Score.

2. Compare to cutoffs developed for the treatment and community samples.

Cutoff scores for the MPSS

Scoring Method	Treatment Sample	Community Sample
Frequency sum	23	15
Severity sum	47	32
Full Scale Score	71	46

Means and Standard Deviations for the two Samples

Sample and Scale	Mean	SD
Treatment Sample		
Frequency sum	23.76	13.16
Severity sum	49.47	18.76
Full Scale Score	79.57	30.51
Community Sample		
Frequency sum	6.15	8.18
Severity	24.61	12.43
Full Scale Score	30.78	20.33

Appendix C

Smyth's *Complete Home-Study Course*

My home-study course for training mental health professionals to treat PTSD by way of the TAB-P protocol is entitled *The TAB-P Protocol: The Complete Home-Study Course for the CBT Exposure-Based Treatment of PTSD and the Other Anxiety Disorders.* The course consists of a study guide and the following six manuals and five videotapes:

Clinicians Manual for the Cognitive-Behavioral Treatment of PTSD and Other Anxiety Disorders—Second Edition. (1999)
ISBN 1-889287-99-7

Clients Manual for the Cognitive-Behavioral Treatment of Anxiety Disorders (1999)
ISBN 1-889287-96-2

Treating Anxiety Disorders with a Cognitive-Behavioral Exposure-Based Approach and the Eye-movement Technique (1996)
The Manual ISBN 1-889287-01-6   The Video ISBN 1-889287-02-4

Titrating Prolonged Exposure with Brief-Exposure Techniques in the Treatment of PTSD and Other Anxiety Disorders (1998)
The Manual ISBN 1-889287-03-2   The Video ISBN 1-889287-04-0

Assimilation Techniques, "Rational" Thinking, and Suppression in the Treatment of PTSD and Other Anxiety Disorders (1998)
The Manual ISBN 1-889287-05-9   The Video ISBN 1-889287-06-7

Applied Relaxation Training in the Treatment of PTSD and Other Anxiety Disorders (1997)
The Manual ISBN 1-889287-07-5   The Video ISBN 1-889287-08-3

The TAB-P Protocol: The Complete Home-Study Course can be purchased from The Red Toad Road Company or New Harbinger Publications.

Visit www.qualityfilmvideo.com/smyth/ or contact the following organizations:

The Red Toad Road Company
P.O. Box 642
Havre de Grace, MD 21078
(410) 939-4092

New Harbinger Publications, Inc.
5674 Shattuck Avenue
Oakland, CA 94609
(800) 748-6273
www.newharbinger.com

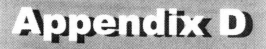

Appendix D

Resources

In addition to my *Complete Home-Study Course* (appendix C) and the works listed in the Works Cited section, the following assessment instruments and texts are very useful. To obtain the instruments, call or write the individuals or organizations listed.

Carlson, E. 1997. *Trauma Assessments*. New York: Guilford Press.

Davidson Trauma Scale (DTS): Call (800) 456-3003 or write to:
Multi-Health Systems, Inc.
908 Niagara Falls Boulevard
North Tonawanda, NY 14120-2060

Deblinger, E., and A. Heflin. 1996. *Treating Sexually Abused Children and Their Non-offending Parents: A Cognitive-Behavioral Approach*. Thousand Oaks, Calif.: Sage.

Meichenbaum, D. 1994. *A Clinical Handbook/Practical Therapist Manual for Assessing and Treating Adults with Post-Traumatic Stress Disorder*. Waterloo, Canada: Institute Press.

Modified PTSD Symptom Scale: Self-Report Version (MPSS-SR): Write to:
Sherry Falsetti
Medical University of South Carolina
Crime Victims Research and Treatment Center
171 Ashley Avenue
Charleston, SC 29425-0742

Posttraumatic Stress Diagnostic Scale (PDS): Call (800) 627-7272, ext. 5151, or write:
National Computer Systems
5605 Green Circle Drive
Minnetanka, MN 55343

PTSD Symptom Scale—Interview (PSS-I): Write to:
    Edna Foa
    Medical College of Pennsylvania
    Department of Psychiatry
    3200 Henry Avenue
    Philadelphia, PA 19129
Structured Interview for PTSD (SI-PTSD): Write to:
    Jonathan Davidson
    Department of Psychiatry
    Box 3812
    Duke University Medical Center
    Durham, NC 27710-3812
Symptom Checklist-90R (SCL-90R) and Brief Symptom Inventory (BSI):
    Call (800) 627-7271, or write to:
    National Computer Systems
    5605 Green Circle Drive
    Minnetanka, MN 55343
Wilson, J., and T. Keane, eds. 1997. *Assessing Psychological Trauma and PTSD.* New York: Guilford Press.

Treatment Plan

Problem: Posttraumatic Stress

Definition: Direct exposure to an extreme traumatic stressor, followed by symptoms that may include intrusive thoughts/memories/images, distressing dreams, reliving anxiety, depression, psychological reactivity, anger outbursts, sleep difficulties, hypervigilance, difficulty concentrating, withdrawal, and avoidance.

Goals: Significant reduction in key symptoms, as well as overall reactivity when exposed to internal or external cues that resemble the original trauma.

Objectives:	**Interventions:**
1. Understanding anxiety.	1. Education regarding the cognitive behavioral model of anxiety and phobia.
2. Develop anxiety-management skills.	2. Introduce the SUDs scale, the "relaxation response," the "eye-movement technique," and "compartmentalization of worry technique."
3. Assimilate the traumatic memories.	3. Introduce Socratic questioning to change "irrational" appraisals, reframe the memory using metaphors.
4. Reduce fear response and avoidance.	4. Imaginal and *in vivo* stress inoculation training, prolonged exposure for desensitization, and coping effects.
5. Maintain treatment gains.	5. Educate regarding relapse-prevention techniques.

Diagnosis: 309.81 Posttraumatic Stress Disorder

Works Cited

Acierno, R., M. Hersen, V. Van Hasselt, and G. Tremont. 1993. Review of the validation and dissemination of eye-movement desensitization and reprocessing. *Clinical Psychology Review* 14, 4:287–299.

Beck, A. 1976. *Cognitive therapy and the emotional disorders*. Madison, Conn: International Universities Press.

Beutler, L. E., P. P. Machado, and S. A. Neufeldt. 1994. Therapist variables. Chap. 7 in *Handbook of psychotherapy and behavior change*. New York: John Wiley & Sons.

Boudewyn, P., S. Stwertka, L. Hyer, W. Albrecht, and E. Sperr. 1993. Eye movement desensitization for PTSD of combat. *Behavior Therapist* 16:29–33.

Breslau, N., G. Davis, P. Andreski, and E. Peterson. 1991. Traumatic events and PTSD in an urban population of young adults. *Archives of General Psychiatry* 48:216–222.

Breslau, N., Kessler, R., Chilcoat, H., Schultz, L., Davis, G., and Andreski, P. 1998. Trauma and posttraumatic stress disorder in the community. *Archives of General Psychiatry*, 55, 626–632.

Brom, D., R. Kleber, and P. Defares. 1989. Brief psychotherapy for PTSD. *Journal of Consulting and Clinical Psychology* 57, 5:607–612.

Chambless, D., and M. Gillis. 1993. Cognitive therapy of anxiety disorders. *Journal of Consulting and Clinical Psychology* 61, 2:248–260.

Chambless, D., et al. 1998. Update on empirically validated therapies, II. *The Clinical Psychologist* 51, 1:3–16.

Clum, G., G. A. Clum, and R. Surls. 1993. A meta-analysis of treatments for panic disorder. *Journal of Consulting and Clinical Psychology* 61, 2:317–326.

Cohen, J., and A. Mannarino. 1996. A treatment outcome study for sexually abused preschoolers. *Journal of the American Academy of Child and Adolescent Psychiatry* 35, 1:42–50.

Courtois, C. 1988. *Healing the incest wound*. New York: W.W. Norton Company.

Creamer, M., P. Burgess, and P. Pattison. 1992. Reaction to trauma. *Journal of Abnormal Psychology* 101:453–459.

Davidson, J., H. Kudler, and R. Smith. 1990. Assessment and pharmocotherapy of posttraumatic stress disorder. In *Biological assessment and treatment of posttraumatic stress disorder*. Washington, D.C.: American Psychiatric Press.

Davidson, J., S. Book, J. Colhet, L. Tupler, S. Roth, D. David, M. Hertzberg, T. Mellman, J. Beckham, R. Smith, R. Davidson, R. Katz, and M. Feldman. 1998. Assessment of a new self-rating scale for post-traumatic stress disorder. *Psychological Medicine*.

Deblinger, E., and A. Heflin. 1996. *Treating sexually abused children and their nonoffending parents*. Thousand Oaks, Calif.: Sage.

Deblinger, E., S. McLeer, and D. Henry. 1990. Cognitive behavioral treatment for sexually abused, physically abused, and nonabused children. *Journal of the American Academy of Child and Adolescent Psychiatry* 29:747–752.

Derogatis, L. R. 1983. SCL-90: *Administration, scoring and procedures manual for the revised version*. Baltimore: Clinical Psychometric Research.

Derogatis, L. R., and N. Melisaratos. 1983. The brief symptom inventory. *Psychological Medicine* 13:595–605.

Dyck, M. 1993. A proposal for a conditioning model of eye movement desensitization treatment for PTSD. *Journal of Behavior Therapy and Experimental Psychiatry* 24:201–210.

Ellis, A. 1975. *A new guide to rational living*. Hollywood: Prentice Hall.

Epstein, S. 1994. Integration of the cognitive and the psychodynamic unconscious. *American Psychologist* 49, 8:709–724.

Falsetti, S., H. Resnick, P. Resnick, and D. Kilpatrick. 1993. The modified PTSD symptom scale. *The Behavioral Therapist* 16:161–162.

Fava, G., S. Grandi, and R. Canestrari. 1991. Mechanisms of change of panic attacks with exposure treatment of agoraphobia. *Journal of Affective Disorders* 22:65–71.

Fava, G., M. Zielezny, G. Savron, and S. Grandi. 1995. Long-term effects of behavioral treatment for panic disorder with agoraphobia. *British Journal of Psychiatry* 166:87–92.

Feske, U. 1998. Eye movement desensitization and reprocessing treatment for PTSD. *Clinical Psychology: Science and Practice* 5, 2:171–181.

Feske, U., and A. Goldstein. 1997. Eye movement desensitization and reprocessing treatment for panic disorder. *Journal of Consulting and Clinical Psychology* 65.6: 1026–1035.

Foa, E. 1996. The efficacy of behavior therapy with obsessive-compulsives. *The Clinical Psychologist* 49, 2:19–22.

Foa, E., and M. Kozak. 1986. Emotional processing of fear. *Psychological Bulletin* 99:20–35.

Foa, E., and D. Riggs. 1993. PTSD in rape victims. In *American psychiatric press review of psychiatry*, vol. 12. Washington, D.C.: American Psychiatric Press.

Foa, E., and B. Rothbaum. 1989. Behavioral psychotherapy for posttraumatic stress disorder. *International Review of Psychiatry* 1(3):219–227.

Foa, E., B. Rothbaum, D. Riggs, T. Murdock. 1991. Treatment of post-traumatic stress disorder in rape victims. *Journal of Consulting and Clinical Psychology* 59(5): 715–723.

Foa, E., D. Riggs, C. Dancu, and B. Rothbaum. 1993. Reliability and validity of a brief instrument for assessing post-traumatic stress disorder. *Journal of Traumatic Stress* 6:459–474.

Frankl, V. 1959. *From death camp to existentialism.* New York: Beacon.

Friedman, M. J. 1988. Toward rational pharmocotherapy for post-traumatic stress disorder. *American Journal of Psychiatry* 145:281–285.

———. 1991. Biological approaches to the diagnosis and treatment of post-traumatic stress disorder. *Journal of Traumatic Stress* 4:67–91.

Garfield, S. L. 1994. Research on client variables in psychotherapy. Chap. 6 in *Handbook of psychotherapy and behavior change*, 190–228. New York: John Wiley & Sons.

Green, B. 1994. Psychosocial research in traumatic stress. *Journal of Traumatic Stress* 7(3):341–362.

Heimberg, R. 1993. Specific issues in the cognitive-behavioral treatment of social phobia. *Journal of Clinical Psychiatry* 54:36–45.

Hekmat, H., S. Groth, and D. Rogers. 1994. Pain ameliorating effect of eye movement desensitization. *Journal of Behavior Therapy and Experimental Psychiatry* 25:121–129.

Herman, J. 1992. *Trauma and recovery.* New York: Basic Books.

———. 1993. Sequelae of prolonged and repeated trauma. In *PTSD: DSM-IV and beyond.* Washington, D.C.: American Psychiatric Association Press.

Horowitz, M. 1986. *Stress response syndromes*, 2d ed. Northvale, N.J.: Aronson.

Keane, T. 1989. Post-traumatic stress disorder. *Behavior Therapy* 20:149–153.

Keane, T., J. Fairbanks, J. Caddell, R. Zimering, and M. Bender. 1985. A behavioral approach to assessing and treating posttraumatic stress disorder in Vietnam veterans. In *Trauma and its wake: The study and treatment of posttraumatic stress disorder.* New York: Brunner/Mazel.

Keane, T., J. Fairbanks, J. Caddell, and R. Zimering. 1989. Implosive (flooding) therapy reduces symptoms of PTSD in Vietnam combat veterans. *Behavior Therapy* 20:245–260

Kilpatrick, D., and H. Resnick. 1993. PTSD associated with exposure to criminal victimization in clinical and community populations. In *PTSD: DSM-IV and beyond.* Washington DC: American Psychiatric Association Press.

Kubany, E., and F. Manke. 1995. Cognitive therapy for trauma-related guilt. *Cognitive and Behavioral Practice* 2:23–61.

Kulka, R., W. Schlenger, J. Fairbanks, R. Hough, B. Jordan, C. Marmar, and D. Weisset. 1990. *Trauma and the Vietnam war generation.* New York: Brunner/Mazel.

Lanyon, R. 1997. Detecting deception. *Clinical Psychology: Science and Practice* 4, 4:377–387.

Littrell, J. 1998. Is the reexperience of painful emotion therapeutic? *Clinical Psychology Review* 18, 1:71–102.

Mahoney, M. 1993. Theoretical developments in the cognitive psychotherapies. *Journal of Consulting and Clinical Psychology* 61, 2:187–193.

Marmar, C. 1991. Brief dynamic psychotherapy of posttraumatic stress disorder. *Psychiatric Annals* 21:405–414.

Marquis, J. 1991. A report on seventy-eight cases treated by eye movement desensitization. *Journal of Behavior Therapy & Experimental Psychiatry* 22, 3:187–192.

Martin, R. 1998. The effect of voluntary eye movements on associations and mood. *Journal of Clinical Psychology* 54, 4:545–553.

McFarlane, A. 1989. The aetiology of post-traumatic morbidity. *British Journal of Psychiatry* 154:221–228.

McNally, R., and L. Shin. 1995. Association of intelligence with severity of PTSD symptoms in Vietnam combat veterans. *American Journal of Psychiatry* 156, 6:936–938.

Meichenbaum, D. 1985. *Stress inoculation training.* New York: Pergamon Press.

———. 1993. Changing conceptions of cognitive behavior modification. *Journal of Consulting and Clinical Psychology* 61, 2:202–204.

———. 1994. *A clinical handbook/practical therapist manual for assessing and treating adults with post-traumatic stress disorder.* Waterloo, Canada: Institute Press.

Muris, P., H. Merchelback, I. Holdrinet, and M. Sysenaar. 1998. Treating children. *Journal of Consulting and Clinical Psychology* 66(1):193–198.

Newman, E., D. Riggs, and S. Roth. 1997. Thematic resolution, PTSD, and complex PTSD. *Journal of Traumatic Stress* 10(2):197–213.

Norris, F. 1992. Epidemiology of trauma. *Journal of Consulting and Clinical Psychology* 60:409–418.

Pitman, R., S. Orr, B. Altman, R. Longpre, and M. Macklin. 1996a. Emotional processing during eye movement desensitization and reprocessing therapy of Vietnam veterans with chronic posttraumatic stress disorder. *Comprehensive Psychiatry* 37:419–429.

Pitman, R., P. Scott, B. Altman, R. Longpre, M. Macklin, M. Michaels, and G. Steketee. 1996b. Emotional processing and outcome of imaginal flooding in Vietnam veterans with chronic PTSD. *Comprehensive Psychiatry* 37:409–418.

Renfry, G., and C. Spates. 1994. Eye movement desensitization. *Journal of Behavior Therapy and Experimental Psychiatry* 25:231–239.

Resick, P. 1993. *Cognitive processing for rape victims.* Newbury Park: Sage.

Richards, D., K. Lovell, and I. Marks. 1994. PTSD. *Journal of Traumatic Stress* 7, 4:669–680.

Robins, C., and A. Hayes. 1993. An appraisal of cognitive therapy. *Journal of Consulting and Clinical Psychology* 61, 2:205–214.

Rogers, C. 1957. The necessary and sufficient conditions of therapeutic personality change. *Journal of Consulting Psychology* 21:95–103.

Rosen, G. 1995. The *Aleution Enterprise* sinking and PTSD. *Professional Psychology: Research and Practice* 26, 1:82–87.

Saunders, B., C. Arata, and D. Kilpatrick. 1990. Development of a crime-related posttraumatic stress disorder scale for women within the SCL-90R. *Journal of Traumatic Stress* 3:439–448.

Shapiro, F. 1989. Eye movement desensitization. *Journal of Behavior Therapy and Experimental Psychiatry* 20, 3:211–217.

———. 1995. *Eye movement desensitization and reprocessing*. New York: Guilford Publications.

Smyth, L. 1994a. *Clinician's manual for the cognitive-behavioral treatment of PTSD*. Baltimore: Red Toad Road Company.

———. 1994b. *Client's manual for the cognitive-behavioral treatment of anxiety disorders*. Baltimore: Red Toad Road Company.

———. 1996b. *Treating anxiety disorders with a cognitive-behavioral exposure based approach and the eye-movement technique: The video*. Baltimore: Red Toad Road Company.

———. 1998a. *Applied relaxation training in the treatment of ptsd and other anxiety disorders: the manual*. Baltimore: Red Toad Road Company.

———. 1998b. *Applied relaxation training in the treatment of ptsd and other anxiety disorders: the video*. Baltimore: Red Toad Road Company.

———. 1998c. *Assimilation, "rational" thinking, and suppression in the treatment of post traumatic stress disorder and other anxiety disorders: The Manual*. Baltimore: Red Toad Road Company.

———. 1998d. *Assimilation, "rational" thinking, and suppression in the treatment of post traumatic stress disorder and other anxiety disorders: The Video*. Baltimore: Red Toad Road Company.

———. 1998e. *Titrating prolonged exposure with brief exposure in the treatment of ptsd and other anxiety disorders: the manual*. Baltimore: Red Toad Road Company.

———. 1998f. *Titrating prolonged exposure with brief exposure in the treatment of ptsd and other anxiety disorders: The Video*. Baltimore: Red Toad Road Company.

Solomon, S., E. Gerrity, and A. Meff. 1992. Efficacy of treatments for posttraumatic stress disorder. *Journal of the American Medical Association*. 268:633–638.

Soloman, S., and E. Smith. 1994. Social support and perceived control as moderators of responses to dioxin and flood exposure. In *Individual and community responses to trauma and disaster*. Ursano, R., B. McCaughey, and C. Fullerton (Eds.) New York: Cambridge University Press.

Speed, N., B. Engdahl, J. Schwart, and R. Eberly. 1991. PTSD as a consequence of the POW experience. *Journal of Nervous and Mental Disease* 177:147–153.

Stampf, T., and D. Levis. 1967. Essentials of implosive therapy. *Journal of Abnormal Psychology* 86: 276–284.

Stauffer, L., and E. Deblinger. 1996. Cognitive behavioral groups for nonoffending mothers and their young sexually abused children. *Child Maltreatment* 1, 1:65–76.

Strong, S. 1978. Social psychological approach to psychotherapy research. In *Handbook of psychotherapy and behavior change*, 2d ed. New York: John Wiley & Sons.

Suinn, R. 1990. *Anxiety management training*. New York: Plenum Press.

Sutherland, S., and J. Davidson. 1994. Pharmacotherapy for posttraumatic stress disorder. *Psychiatric Clinics of North America* 17, 2:409–423.

Tallis, F., and E. Smith. 1994. Does rapid eye movement desensitization facilitate emotional processing? *Behavior Research and Therapy* 32:459–461.

Thase, M., A. Simons, and J. McGeary. 1992. Relapse after cognitive behavior therapy of depression. *American Journal of Psychiatry* 149:1046–1052.

True, W., J. Rise, S. Eisen, A. Heath, J. Goldberg, M. Lyonsl, and J. Nowak. 1993. A twin study of genetic and environmental contributions to liability for posttraumatic stress symptoms. *Archives of General Psychiatry* 50:257–264.

van der Kolk, B. 1984. *Post traumatic stress disorder*. Washington, D.C.: American Psychiatric Press.

Van Etten, M., and S. Taylor. 1998. Comparative efficacy of treatments for posttraumatic stress dosorder. *Clinical Psychology and Psychotherapy* 5:126–144.

Vargas, M., and J. Davidson. 1993. Post-traumatic stress disorder. *Psychopharmacology* 16:737–748.

Weathers, F., L. Brett, T. Keane, D. Herman, H. Steinberg, J. Huska, and H. Kraemer. 1996. The utility of the SCL-90R for the diagnosis of war-zone-related PTSD. *Journal of Traumatic Stress* 9, 1:111–128.

Wegner, D., and R. Erber. 1992. The hyperaccessibility of suppressed thoughts. *Journal of Personality and Social Psychology* 63, 6:903–912.

Wegner, D., D. Schneider, S. Carter, and L. White. 1987. Paradoxical effects of thought suppression. *Journal of Personality and Social Psychology* 53:5–13.

Weinberger, J. 1995. Common factors aren't so common. *Clinical Psychology: Science and Practice* 2, 1:45–74.

Weiss, J. 1993. *How psychology works*. New York: Guilford.

Wenzlaff, R., D. Wegner, and D. Roper. 1988. Depression and mental control. *Journal of Personality and Social Psychology* 55, 6:882–892.

Whiston, S., and T. Sexton. 1993. An overview of psychotherapy outcome research. *Professional Psychology: Research and Practice* 24, 1:43–51.

Williams, S. 1990. Guided mastery treatment of agoraphobia. *Progress in Behavior Modification* 26:89–121.

Williams, S., and G. Zane. 1997. Guided mastery treatment of phobias. *The Clinical Psychologist* 50, 2:13–15.

Wolpe, J. 1958. *Psychotherapy by reciprocal inhibition*. Stanford, Calif.: Stanford University Press.

Wolpe, J., and J. Abrams. 1991. Post-traumatic stress disorder overcome by eye-movement desensitization. *Journal of Behavior Therapy and Experimental Psychiatry* 22, 1:39–43.

Yehuda, R., and A. McFarlane. 1994. Conflict between current knowledge about PTSD and its original conceptual basis. *American Journal of Psychiatry* 152, 12: 1705–1713.

Some Other
New Harbinger Titles

Surviving Your Borderline Parent, Item 3287 $14.95

When Anger Hurts, second edition, Item 3449 $16.95

Calming Your Anxious Mind, Item 3384 $12.95

Ending the Depression Cycle, Item 3333 $17.95

Your Surviving Spirit, Item 3570 $18.95

Coping with Anxiety, Item 3201 $10.95

The Agoraphobia Workbook, Item 3236 $19.95

Loving the Self-Absorbed, Item 3546 $14.95

Transforming Anger, Item 352X $10.95

Don't Let Your Emotions Run Your Life, Item 3090 $17.95

Why Can't I Ever Be Good Enough, Item 3147 $13.95

Your Depression Map, Item 3007 $19.95

Successful Problem Solving, Item 3023 $17.95

Working with the Self-Absorbed, Item 2922 $14.95

The Procrastination Workbook, Item 2957 $17.95

Coping with Uncertainty, Item 2965 $11.95

The BDD Workbook, Item 2930 $18.95

You, Your Relationship, and Your ADD, Item 299X $17.95

The Stop Walking on Eggshells Workbook, Item 2760 $18.95

Conquer Your Critical Inner Voice, Item 2876 $15.95

The PTSD Workbook, Item 2825 $17.95

Hypnotize Yourself Out of Pain Now!, Item 2809 $14.95

The Depression Workbook, 2nd edition, Item 268X $19.95

Beating the Senior Blues, Item 2728 $17.95

Shared Confinement, Item 2663 $15.95

Handbook of Clinical Psychopharmacology for Therpists, 3rd edition, Item 2698 $55.95

Getting Your Life Back Together When You Have Schizophrenia, Item 2736 $14.95

Do-It-Yourself Eye Movement Technique for Emotional Healing, Item 2566 $13.95

Call **toll free, 1-800-748-6273,** or log on to our online bookstore at **www.newharbinger.com** to order. Have your Visa or Mastercard number ready. Or send a check for the titles you want to New Harbinger Publications, Inc., 5674 Shattuck Ave., Oakland, CA 94609. Include $4.50 for the first book and 75¢ for each additional book, to cover shipping and handling. (California residents please include appropriate sales tax.) Allow two to five weeks for delivery.

Prices subject to change without notice.

BEST PRACTICES FOR THERAPY

Each of the protocols in this series presents a session-by-session, research-based treatment plan, including evaluation instruments, sample treatment summaries for use with managed care, handouts, weekly homework, and strategies to use for delivering key information. A client manual is available for each protocol, containing all the materials that the client will need.

Overcoming Agoraphobia and Panic Disorder
A 12- to 16-session treatment. By Elke Zuercher-White, Ph.D.

> Therapist protocol, *item 1462* $29.95
> Client manual, *item 1470* $15.95
> Client pack—set of five client manuals, $39.95

Overcoming Depression
A 10-session treatment. By Gary Emery, Ph.D.

> Therapist protocol, *Item 1608* $29.95
> Clent manual, *item 1616* $15.95
> Client pack—set of five client manuals, $39.95

Overcoming Generalized Anxiety Disorder
A 10- to 13-session treatment. By John White, Ph.D.

> Therapist protocol, *item 1446* $29.95
> Client manual, *item 1454* $15.95.
> Client pack—set of five client manuals, $39.95.

Overcoming Obsessive-Compulsive Disorder
A 14-session treatment. By Gail Steketee, Ph.D.

> Therapist protocol, *item 1284* $29.95
> Client manual. *item 1292* $15.95
> Client pack—set of five client manuals, $39.95

Overcoming Post-Traumatic Stress Disorder
A 15-session (or less) treatment. By Larry Smyth, Ph.D.

> Therapist protocol, *item 1624* $29.95
> Client manual, *item 1632* $15.95
> Client pack—set of five client manuals, $39.95

Overcoming Specific Phobia
A 10-session treatment. By Edmund J. Bourne, Ph.D.

> Therapist protocol, *item 1144* $29.95
> Client manual, *item 1152* $15.95
> Client pack—set of five client manuals, $39.95

Overcoming Situational and General Anger
A 9-session treatment. By Jerry L. Deffenbacher, Ph.D., and Matthew McKay, Ph.D.

> Therapist protocol, *item 1144* $29.95
> Client manual, *item 1152* $15.95
> Client pack—set of five client manuals, $39.95

Call toll-free 1-800-748-6273 to order. Have your Visa or Mastercard number ready. Or send a check for the titles you want to New Harbinger Publications, 5674 Shattuck Avenue, Oakland, CA 94609. Include $4.50 for the first item and 75¢ for each additional item to cover shipping and handling. (California residents please include appropriate sales tax.) Allow four to six weeks for delivery.

Prices subject to change without notice.

CPSIA information can be obtained at www.ICGtesting.com
Printed in the USA
BVOW050935100912

300039BV00003B/1/A